FEMALE FOETICIDE
Myth and Reality

*374 case histories of women
who have undergone female foeticide
in Punjab, India*

FEMALE FOETICIDE
Myth and Reality

*374 case histories of women
who have undergone female foeticide
in Punjab, India*

ANURAG AGARWAL

STERLING PUBLISHERS PRIVATE LIMITED

STERLING PUBLISHERS PRIVATE LIMITED
A-59 Okhla Industrial Area, Phase-II, New Delhi-110020.
Tel: 26386209; 26387070, Fax: 91-11-26383788
E-mail: ghai@nde.vsnl.net.in
www.sterlingpublishers.com

Female Foeticide: Myth and Reality
© 2003, Anurag Agarwal
ISBN 81 207 2574 3

All rights are reserved. No part of this publication may be reproduced, stored in a retrieval system or transmitted, in any form or by any means, mechanical, photocopying, recording or otherwise, without prior written permission of the original publisher.

PRINTED IN INDIA

Published by Sterling Publishers Pvt. Ltd., New Delhi-110 020.
Laserset at Vikas Compographics, New Delhi-110020.
Printed at Rastra Rachna Printer, Delhi.

*To
my mother
Mithlesh Gupta*

Acknowledgements

This study would not have been possible without the efforts of 500 volunteers of ISS — Istri Sehat Sabhas (Women Health Groups) who interviewed women who had undergone female foeticide.

My first debt is to Mr T. Nawaz, team leader of the World Bank Project and Dr P. Kudesia, Senior Health Adviser, World Bank for their overall support and encouragement.

I also owe a debt of gratitude to Mrs J.K.Bawa, State Health Media Coordinator and Dr Rupinder Walia who sensitised, motivated and trained the volunteers of Istri Sehat Sabhas by holding District Level Workshops and training camps.

I am thankful to Mr Jagjit Singh, System Analyst and Mr Vinay Gupta, Application Supervisor, Punjab Health Systems Corporation for developing the software and for their help in generating the reports.

Dr Usha Adya, Assistant Director, Punjab Health Systems Corporation and Dr Dalbir Kaur, Clinical Psychologist, developed the questionnaire and did the field testing. Their contribution is invaluable.

The difficult task of data entry was successfully carried out by computer operators, Ms Arshinder, Ms Jyotsana, Ms Puja, Ms Ritu, Ms Pushpa, Ms Kalpana and Ms Nirupma. My heart felt-thanks are due to all of them.

Finally, I want to thank all those who helped me in drafting and editing the text.

Contents

Acknowledgements   vi

Preface   ix

1. **Female Foeticide and Sex Ratio**   1
   - 1.1 Introduction
   - 1.2 Misuse of Reproductive Technology
   - 1.3 Gender Bias
   - 1.4 Indian Sex Ratio
   - 1.5 Why Male Preference is Particularly Dominant in Punjab?
   - 1.6 A Mathematical Formulation
   - 1.7 Social Dimensions of the Problem

2. **The Study**   9
   - 2.1 Need for the Present Study
   - 2.2 Objective of the Study
   - 2.3 Mode of Survey
   - 2.4 Methodology
   - 2.5 Training of Istri Sehat Sabhas (Women Health Groups)
   - 2.6 Survey

3. **Case Studies**   12

4. **Analysis**   26
   - 4.1 Computerisation of the Data
   - 4.2 Results and Observations
   - 4.3 Statistical Test – Chi Square Test
   - 4.4 Summary and Conclusion

Annexure I: 77
    Filled in Questionnaire in Punjabi

Annexure II: 84
    Questionnaire in English

Annexure III: 91
    Front End Forms

Preface

Punjab has one of the most adverse sex ratios in the country. Overall sex ratio in the state is 874 females per 1000 males and it shows further declining trend in the children. Sex ratios for the age groups of 0-6 years and 0-1 years are 793 and 747, respectively. Through abuse of ultrasound scanning, parents are going for sex selective abortions. Every year more than one hundred thousand female foetuses are killed in Punjab.

The book is based on the inerviews of 374 females who had undergone female foeticide. These interviews based on comprehensive questionnaire were taken by the volunteers of Istri Sehat Sabhas (Women Healh Groups). To undersand the psyche of these women, quantitative tools were applied to analyse how certain socio economic factors such as caste, education, financial well being, etc affect the thinking and perception of these women.

The findings of the study negate many of the common beliefs and perceptions strongly held by most of us. For example, there is strong religious advocacy on this issue based on the presumption that women who undergo female foeticide do not realise that it is a sin and if they were made to realise it, they would not commit the sin of female foeticide. The reality is that 85% of the women who had undergone female foeticide already had the realisation that it was a sin. This is the reason why the present form of religious advocacy has not worked.

Gender bias is the interplay of various socio-economic factors and is deeply rooted in our mindset. Modern medical technology has worked as a catalyst to metamorphose strong preference for a male child, with desire for a small family, into female foeticide. In this book I have tried to give an insight into the psyche of the women who had undergone female foeticide, which is essential to have any successful strategy to combat this menace.

1

Female Foeticide and Sex Ratio

1.1 Introduction

The principle of gender equality has been basic to Indian thinking for over a century. The nineteenth and twentieth centuries saw a succession of women's movements around burning social issues — from women's education and widow re-marriage to the freedom struggle itself. Women from all walks of life participated actively in the freedom struggle by responding to the call of Mahatma Gandhi, a champion of women's rights. The Constitution of India guarantees equality to women. It empowers the state to adopt measures for affirmative discrimination in favour of women and also imposes a fundamental duty on its citizens to uphold the dignity of women.

But despite all these, India's deep-rooted 'sons only' ethos continues. Our ancient texts such as Manusmriti did place the man on a higher pedestal than the women. But our heritage asks us to pay the highest regard to women. The religious teachings in the Vedas, Puranas and epics like Ramayana and Mahabharata did not at any time discriminate against the female. Our scriptures speak of Lakshmi, Saraswati and Durga, the ultimate source of power. Our history speaks of Maitreyee and Arundhati. It was perhaps the consequence of repeated invasions and subjugations, especially atrocities committed on local women by victorious invaders that women began to be perceived as a liability in society. This explains why states in northwestern India, which faced the brunt of most invasions, display almost the most adverse sex ratio.

During the twentieth century, census operations began. In 1901 the sex ratio was 972 women per 1000 males, which fell to 941 women per 1000 males in 1961, and 927 women per 1000 males in 1991. The census of 2001 further highlights how little women are valued in the country.

1.2 Misuse of Reproductive Technology

New developments in the medical technology have helped improve healthcare for millions of people. One cheap and widely available test can tell the sex of the unborn child. Through abuse of ultrasound imaging, parents tend to be calculative in choosing the sex of their child. It is an unfortunate example of misuse of modern technology.

There is rampant misuse of reproductive technology in a society characterised by a strong bias against the female child. This new-sophisticated reproductive technology was first introduced in India in mid 70s. Amniocentesis was introduced for diagnostic value. The technique was to help couples running the risk of giving birth to genetically deformed child. The aspect of sex determination technique caught the attention of the doctors in India, as they foresaw its enormous potential for the son besotted Indian society. Soon thousands of sex determination clinics sprang up in all parts of the country. Doctors offered hope to couples wanting to have son, leading to sex selective abortions and a fall in the population of girls. Millions of female foetusses are mercilessly killed every year by their parents under the most sophisticated prenatal diagnostic techniques.

Now, more sophisticated methods have hit the market. The Ericsson method, for example, separates the X and Y-chromosomes from the sperm and then injects back only the Y chromosomes into the womb to ensure a boy. It costs Rs.15,000 to 20,000 to the couple and spares them to go through sex selective abortion.

The pre-implantation genetic diagnosis (PGD) helps to determine the sex of even an unrecognisable foetus. As early as three days after fertilization, one or two cells are removed from an 8-10 celled embryo, which is then re-implanted into the uterus. Its high cost, Rs. 100,000 per treatment cycle, is a deterrent.

It is ironical that these sex determination techniques and facilities have reached even remote villages. These techniques have widened the gender gap that exists in various areas of our social and economic life. It is a technological revolution of a reactionary kind.

1.3 Gender Bias

Gender bias is deeply rooted in the Indian psyche. The popular perception draws the girl child as a losing proposition — only to be married into another family. This leads to natural dislike for girls. The society looks down upon female child as a liability and male child as an asset. The fear of dowry on the one hand and losing property in inheritance on the other are major irritants in acceptance of a girl child.

Neglect of female infants and better health care for males is another reason accounting for the decline in sex ratio. Discrimination against female children starts early, and is maintained as the female child grows. A critical manifestation of this discrimination is the under allocation of medicine and food to the female offspring. This gender bias in the allocation of critical life-sustaining resources appears to be the mechanism that gives rise to gender differences in mortality.

Indian women also face ingrained discrimination because the value of their labour is neither accounted for in official statistics nor appreciated by policy-makers. Women's work, no matter how rigorous, taxing or draining, is considered part of their duty, undeserving of compensation. And Indian women work at least 10 to 12 hours daily, two hours more than the average for men.

1.4 Indian Sex Ratio

Biologically for every 100 girls, 105 boys are born. In the first year after birth, through higher death rates among boys, the figures even out. So logically for 1000 women there should be 1000 men – UNICEF

As per 2001 census, the national all-age sex ratio (the number of females for every thousand males) at 933 represents an improvement of six points compared with 927 in the 1991 census. Although this reflects a reversal of the declining sex ratio in many decades, it is nowhere near the figure of 972 – recorded way back in the 1901 census. However, the "natural sex ratio" should be above 1,000. Socio-cultural factors impinge to distort the natural sex numbers. According to United Nations, the world estimate of sex ratio in 2000 is 986 females per 1000 males.

Sex Ratio of India from 1901 to 2001

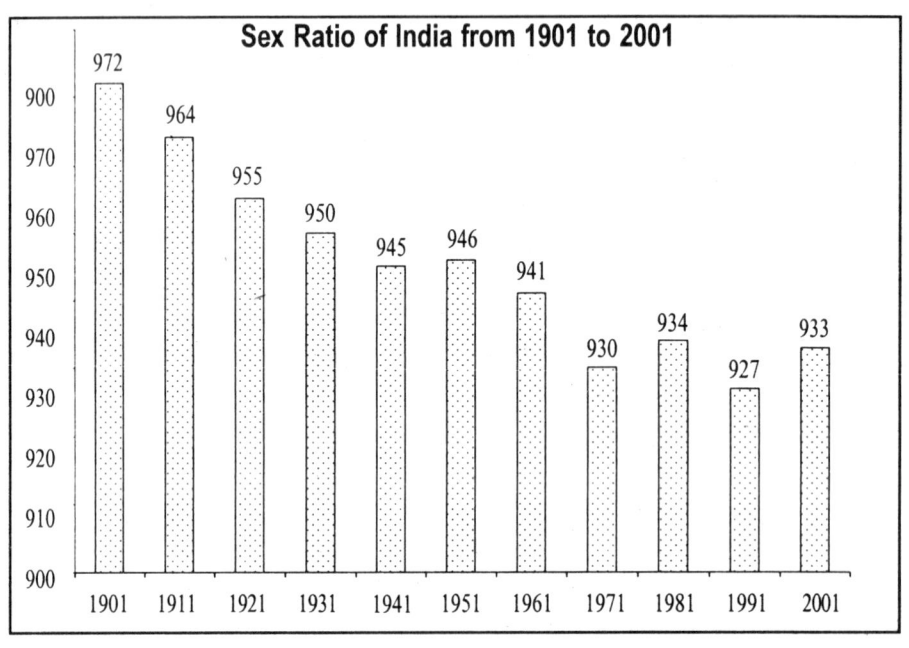

Year	1901	1911	1921	1931	1941	1951	1961	1971	1981	1991	2001
Ratio	972	964	955	950	945	946	941	930	934	927	933

Graph-I

Data from India's 2001 census shows the sex ratio for 0-6 year fell from 945 females per 1,000 males in 1991 to 927 in 2001. The implications of the drop in sex ratio in the 0-6 age group would be immense for the country. It might prove difficult to handle the situation a few years from now.

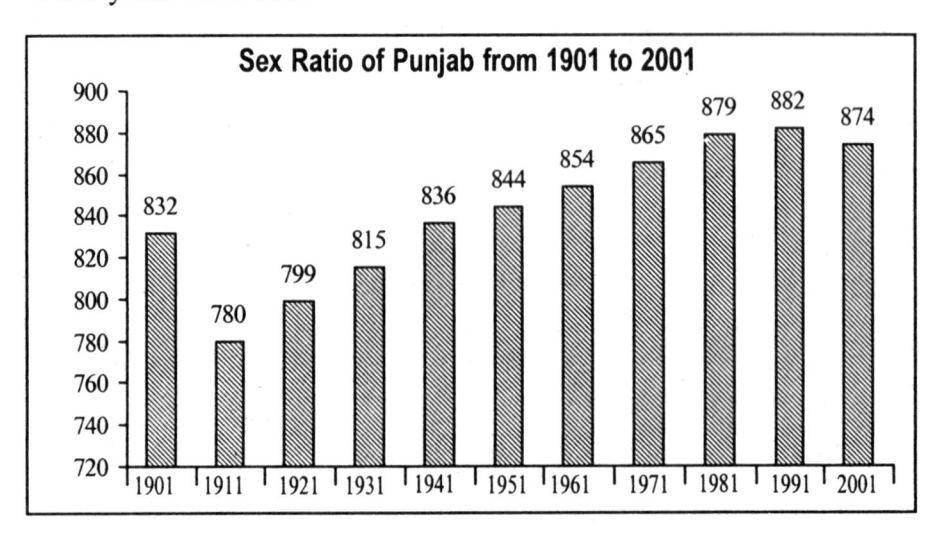

Sex Ratio of Punjab from 1901 to 2001

Year	1901	1911	1921	1931	1941	1951	1961	1971	1981	1991	2001
Ratio	832	780	799	815	836	844	854	865	879	882	874

Graph-II

In 1991, two states had child sex ratios below 880. Today, there are five states and union territories in this category: Punjab (793), Haryana (820), Chandigarh (845) Delhi (865) and Gujarat (878). The Punjab-Haryana-Himachal Pradesh belt in the north is called by some 'India's Bermuda Triangle' - where girls vanish without a trace.

Scenario in Punjab

As per the latest 2001 census, a significant feature of Punjab population is preponderance of males over females. Out of a total population of 24,289,296 in the state, 12,963,362 are males and 11,325,934 are females, resulting in low sex ratio. Historically Punjab has had the most adverse sex ratio in the country. The situation has further deteriorated in 2001. It is to be noted that the sex ratio in Punjab was consistently rising

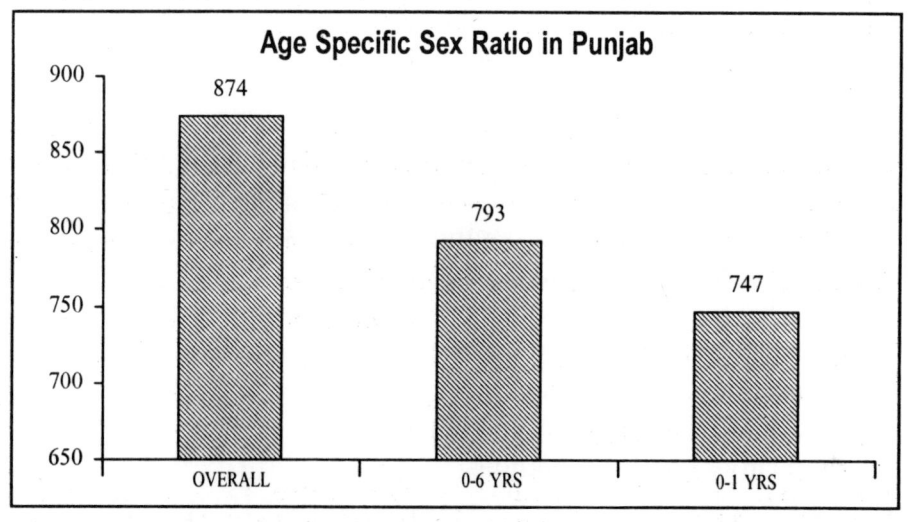

Graph-III

from 1911 till 1991. But after so many years, it showed a decline from 882 in 1991 to 874 in 2001.

It is to be noted that age-specific sex ratios in Punjab are shocking and reflect the most adverse sex ratio. Considering the overall sex ratio of 874, the ratios in 0-6 and 0-1 years show a very disturbing downward trend.

For the sex ratio to confirm female foeticide, the sex ratios at birth need to be analysed. From the data of birth registration, the sex ratio of births in the year 2001 is 747.

Sex ratio of Punjab in age group 0-1 & 0-6

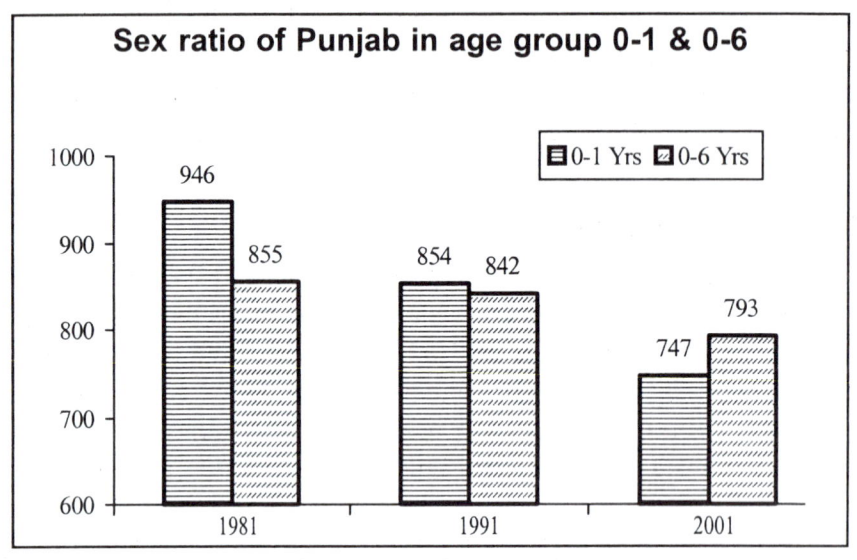

Year	0-1 Yrs	0-6 Yrs
1981	946	855
1991	854	842
2001	747	793

Graph-IV

There is a rapidly steep worsening of 0-6 and 0-1 age group sex ratios in Punjab in the last 30 years when compared with national figures.

The downward trend is continuing and is amplified clearly in Graph-IV, which shows worsening sex ratio in infants in these age groups. This trend can be explained by the following facts:
- increase in number of sex determination clinics
- decreasing cost of this test
- social acceptability of the issue
- relative safety of abortions

1.5 Why Male Preference is Particularly Dominant in Punjab?

According to 2001 census, every fifth female child in Punjab is missing. The preference for a male child is particularly pronounced in Punjab, because of its martial and agricultural traditions. Punjab has always demanded sons who could go into battle or plough fields during peace time. The following reasons aggravate the decline in the sex ratio.

1. The concept of purity of identity and evolution of Sikhs as a "martial race" has contributed to strong preference for male child, which has now metamorphosed into female foeticide.

2. Punjab being border state of India was prone to external invasions. More males were needed to go into battle, fight wars, protect their lands and women.
3. Over the years, the peasant society has imposed a hierarchy that emanates from the land holdings structure. With the success of green revolution, the value of land increased, and thereby increasing the value of male offspring.
4. Militancy in 1980s reinforced the traditional bias for a son. The period of terrorism accentuated the attitudes of viewing the girl as a liability.
5. Centuries of social customs like daughters have to be protected and given away in marriage with dowry.

1.6 A Mathematical Formulation

Let us see what sex ratio we are heading for? Since Punjab is a progressive state, most of the families want to have only two children. Furthermore, they also desire to have at least one male child in the family.

Let us calculate what sex ratio a society would have if it follows the family norm of "two children with at least one male"

Assumption - Probability (male) = probability (female)

Therefore sex ratio - 4F/4M = 1; that is 1,000 females per 1,000 males.

The four situations as mentioned below are responsible for maintaining the natural sex ratio. Thus, biological sex ratio will be maintained as 1000.

Possibilities					Possibilities				
Children	1	2	3	4	Children	1	2	3	4
1	M	M	F	F	1	M	M	F	F
2	M	F	M	(F)	2	M	F	M	(M)

However, medical technology intervenes at the possibility no.4. It changes second female child to male child in the fourth possibility. The intervention in natural birth order is depicted in favour of male births.

Therefore sex ratio - 3F/5M = 0.6; that is 600 females per 1,000 males. This is what Punjab is heading for!

1.7 Social Dimensions of the Problem

In mad pursuit of a male child, we might be risking our future. The society is heading for a dangerous situation. Estimates suggest that at least 5 million female foeticide operations are conducted every year in the country. Female foeticide has its roots in social attitudes. If unchecked, foeticide may eventually permanently damage the demographic balance in India. Upsetting the delicate balance will prove to be catastrophic. It will haunt the country for generations.

It will lead to violence against women. Sexual offences against women will disturb the social fiber of society and change the value systems.

2

The Study

2.1 Need for the Present Study

Many studies have been conducted on gender bias, on female foeticide by collecting data from doctors and other secondary sources. Some NGOs have done studies on the reasons for female foeticide but they are based on the opinions of the medical professionals, gatekeepers of the society and, in few cases, family members of the lady who had undergone this procedure. But little has been done to understand the psyche of the women who undergo female foeticide.

Moreover, in most of these studies only subjective analysis is done based on few case histories. It is important to look at this problem objectively to have a good understanding of social, religious, economic and emotional factors, which have built gender bias in the mindset of the mothers. Considering these factors, a community based qualitative survey/study was undertaken in the rural, and semi urban population of Punjab.

2.2 Objective of the Study

The main objective of the study is : *To understand the psyche of women who have undergone female foeticide.*

In this study only cases of female foeticide have been taken. In all these cases sex determination was done with the help of ultrasound scanning followed by abortion, in case the foetus was a female. The study has excluded cases of simple abortion where lady had undergone abortion due to medical reasons or unwanted pregnancy. It is a very focussed study on female foeticide and does not cover other aspects of gender bias. The objective of the study is not to come out with any policy or strategy to combat the menace of female foeticide, it is only an attempt to read the mind of the mothers who had undergone this act. I have tried to analyse, how certain socio-economic parameters such as education, financial status of the family, religious status, caste, religion, level of decision making of the lady in the family, affect the perception and thinking of these women.

2.3 Mode of Survey

To understand why a woman has undergone female foeticide, it was essential to interview her. Since it is a very personal and confidential information, which no woman would share with an outsider, it was necessary that the interviewer should be from that village only. The survey was undertaken with the help of grass-root voluntary workers of ISS – Istri Sehat Sabhas (Women Health Groups), in the villages.

Istri Sehat Sabha (ISS) is a voluntary women group in most of the villages and slum areas of Punjab. It comprises of 10 members representing all strata of the community. These members meet every month and discuss local specific health problems.

There are about 5,000 Istri Sehat Sabhas in Punjab.

2.4 Methodology

A. **Survey Area:** The survey area covered all the 17 districts of Punjab.

B. **Sample Size:** To build up the sampling frame, 500 women who had already undergone female foeticide were selected by the ISS. The study was conducted over a period of 3 months from November 2001 to January 2002.

C. **Tool:** A questionnaire was designed to have indepth interaction with the respondents. The questionnaire also focused on the social, religious, economic and emotional angle of respondents.

D. **Data Collection:** Active members of the ISS were selected as interviewers. One-day orientation-cum-training camps were organised for them. These orientation trainings were conducted in Chandigarh as well as at the district level in a phased manner covering 2-3 districts at one

The Study 11

- At least 5 ISS members from each block of a given district participated in this training. They were accompanied by MPHW – Multipurpose Health Workers (Female).
- Each nominated delegate was at least a matriculate; active in social work and influential in her neighbouhood.
- They were imparted training on conducting the desired survey in their village under the supervision of concerned ANM/MPHW (Female)

2.5 Training of ISS

Training was conducted for the ISS members before survey. It involved:

i) Active interactive sessions with the members for their views on female foeticide
ii) Sensitisation to the issue
iii) Introduction of questionnaire
iv) Mock interviews and group discussions

Pre-testing of questionnaire was done and it was revised accordingly.

All ISS members were explained that a complete anonymity and confidentiality of the women is to be maintained. At no place they should refer the name, address of the women and this fact should also be explained to them. Respondents should be reassured that only statistical information will be used.

2.6 Survey

Each ISS member conducted the interview of women in her village who had undergone female foeticide.

All the case histories recorded on the proforma were scrutinised at the HQ. After going through the recorded data, only 374 case histories were considered for the study. Rest of the cases had to be rejected due to incomplete information. This was because some of the ISS workers who took the interview as well as the respondents were not well educated. Even in the selected 374 case histories, information in few columns is missing, but this is not critical information, especially where interviewer was to fill in specific reasons for a response. For example, almost all filled in the information that, whether according to the respondent society gives preference to the boys or not, but many did not fill in specific reasons for the same.

3

Case Studies

The information presented in this study has been based on the survey data compiled from the raw information generated through completion of a specifically designed questionnaire (Annexure I and II). During the survey, identity of the respondent was not captured. Names given to the respondents in the following cases are fictitious. A total of 500 questionnaires were distributed to the volunteers of Women Health Groups (Istri Sehat Sabhas) to interview the subjects (i.e. women who underwent female foeticide) of their area of operation. After careful scrutiny of the case histories of these subjects and of the data available therefrom, the sample was short listed to 374. The questionnaires (126) giving incomplete and deficient information were not considered. The respondents represented rural as well as semi urban areas of all the 17 districts of the state. Maximum number of case histories were in districts of Amritsar (66), followed by Hoshiarpur(45), Mansa(42), Ropar(35), Faridkot (27) while the minimum was in Kapurthala (3).

The study revealed very interesting state of affairs with respect to the menace of female foeticide in the state. It negates some common views held strongly by most of us. Some selected case studies are given below:

Case 1

Hailing from Bhunga village of Hoshiarpur district, Madhu Bala, a thirty five years old housewife with primary education, married for 14 years with an equally educated man, having a small land holding of 4 kanals only, is living in a joint family. This woman, belonging to a non-religious Saini family, having two daughters of 6 and 12 years, conceived five times, miscarried once and underwent 4-month foeticide

Case Studies

abortion twice. She was of the opinion that only two children (one male and one female) were enough as bigger family often leads to financial hardships. Her desire for a male child took this woman to some quacks/sadhus, who treated her with some desi medication, but of no use. Although this lady was aware of the ultrasound scanning facility of prenatal sex determination, yet believed that it was nature that, by and large, determined whether one conceives a male or a female child. She learnt about this scanning facility from advertisements, friends and relatives that motivated her to go in for female foeticide. Although she had an anxiety before going in for the foeticide operation, yet she yielded to the pressure of her husband, as she had conceived a female child. She felt herself guilty after getting female foeticide operation done. Moreover, this operation affected her health deleteriously in terms of pain in lumber region and general weakness. She saw no good reason in meting out discrimination against the girl child in society. She was, however, conscious that in certain homes, woman giving birth to a male child gets better treatment, in terms of healthier food and improved health care, as she is to rear the male child, which is considered important for the perpetuation of the family tree. Therefore, this woman believed that, if she were blessed with a male child, she would become indifferent for the second issue. She remembers the ill treatment she received from her in-laws for not giving birth to a male child.

Hence, female foeticide is linked to social (family preference for a male child) and economic (desire to keep family size limited due to increasing dearness) reasons.

Case 2

Channo Devi is a schedule caste Sikh from Mansa district which is the most backward area of Punjab. She and her husband are illiterate and landless labourers. She is from a very poor family and lives in a kucha house. She is not very religious and visits gurudwara once in a month. She has three daughters who are 6, 5 and 3 years old. According to her, the ideal family is of one son and one daughter. She thinks that a son is a must in the family. She has been pregnant five times and got female foeticide done twice. She thinks sex of the child depends on God and came to know about ultrasound through her neighbour. She says that it is better to know the sex of the foetus, because it is very essential to have a son, as he looks after the parents in old age. She can decide what to cook because she does not live in a joint family, but for other family and personal decisions, she consults her husband. According to her, first child should be a male and she thinks had it been the case with her, she would not have given birth to so many daughters. She was physically abused by her in-laws for not giving birth to a son. Strong desire for a son took her to one sadhu who gave her a *taweez*, but that also did not help her. She got the abortion done on the advice of her husband and she has no regrets. Though she is 34 years old, she still plans to give any number of chances to have a male child but she does not want to have any more daughter, therefore, she plans to go for sex determination and abortion, in case the foetus is female.

Chhano Devi is illiterate and non-religious but she still thinks that it is a sin to kill the foetus, but this does not deter her from selective abortions.

In such cases, religious advocacy in the present form is not going to work.

Case 3

Gurwinder Kaur, 35 years old, employed woman belonging to an upper caste Jat Sikh family, living in a village of Hoshiarpur District, is married to a graduate employed man belonging to an upper middle class family owning 8 acres of land and a well built pucca house with all facilities including that of electricity, cooking gas, television, scooter, car, radio, etc. She lives with her husband and has a seven-year-old daughter.

Gurwinder Kaur has been pregnant 3 times. Once she got her feotus aborted, because it was a female and once she had a miscarriage. She believed that an ideal family size is one son and one daughter. She is aware of the ultrasound scanning facilities for the determination of sex of the unborn baby. She came to know about the ultrasound technology from the advertisements and newspapers. She agrees that there is strong male preference in the society because sons carry family name. Giving birth to a male child increases the status of the woman in the society, and the mother is better looked after during her pregnancy. A lady giving birth to a male child gets better respect and treatment from her in-laws and she is better looked after in terms of food and health care. She is not a religious lady. She underwent the four months female foeticide operation

Case Studies

under her own motivation, and that of her husband and in-laws. She feels female foeticide is the biggest sin and deeply regrets having done it. She disclosed one of their relatives also underwent female foeticide operation, because they already had two daughters and did not want the third one as they had a strong desire to get a male child. She thinks that she is indifferent to the sex of her first issue, but if she does not get the male child, she would go in for conception four more times.

Though not religious, she thinks that female foeticide is a sin and regrets it, but wants to try four more times for a male child.

Case 4

Manjit is a 25 year old matriculate, with an equally educated husband residing in Ludhiana, an industrial district of Punjab. She belongs to a medium class family, living with her in-laws and is of Jat Sikh caste. She is married for 9 years and has only one living daughter. Her second daughter expired immediately after birth due to some medical problem, thereafter, she has undergone 3 abortions after it showed in ultrasonography as girl. She rightly knows that husband is responsible for the sex of the foetus and came to know about ultrasound technology from her in-laws. She thinks that this technology is not good as after knowing the sex of the unborn child the whole period of pregnancy is wrought with mental tensions if the child is female. According to her, the ideal family should comprise of a son and a daughter and the first born child can be of any sex, but should be of sound health. She blames her mother-in-law for instigating her husband to force her to undergo foeticide. On behest of her mother-in-law, she was threatened by her husband to be left at her parental place, if she does not bear a son for him as all his brothers have a son. She was also physically abused by her husband. She feels that her sisters-in-law who have sons have more say in the family than her and she is often subjected to taunts. She admits that her social status is dismal and bearing a son would give her a more secure and happy life. She was also taken to some sadhu/mahatma by her mother-in law who blessed her by giving some fruit so that she may bear a son, but inspite of that she conceived a female and had to get it aborted. She herself never wanted to go in for abortions and feels guilty about it, but because of ill-treatment meted out to her by her husband and in-laws, she was forced to commit the sin of foeticide.

Case 5

Rupinder is a teacher in a middle school in Ropar district. She is 34 years old, married for 14 years. She and her husband both are graduates and have basic households, such as, pucca house, electricity, television, vehicle. She is a very religious Khatri Sikh and lives in a joint family with her husband's elder brother's family. She has two daughters though, according to her, ideal family size is one son and one daughter. She got female foeticide done only once, when she was 3 ½ months pregnant. Though she is a teacher but still thinks that sex of the child depends on God. She came to know about ultrasound scanning through advertisements in newspapers. She strongly feels that the preference given to male child by the society is wrong and attitude of the society towards female must change. She is an empowered woman who can take almost all family decisions, including when to go to her parents and when to conceive. According to her, first child can be anyone, male or female and she is against sex determination, because then pregnancy is full of tension and also there is pressure for getting it aborted, in case it is female. She says that it was her own decision to go in for female foeticide. The reason she gave was that her husband has only one brother who has three daughters and she has two daughters, so there are only daughters in the family. Therefore, she had a strong desire to have a male child in their joint family. After abortion she had weakness for few months and now she regrets having undergone abortion and thinks that foeticide is a big sin. Now she is not planning for any other child and in case she gets pregnant she would not go for sex determination.

A teacher, who went for female foeticide on her own, is now determined not to repeat it. She holds strong views against gender bias prevalent in the society.

Case 6

Charanjit Kaur, of Multania village of Bathinda district, is a twenty-eight years old illiterate housewife, married for 9 years to a man with 5th standard education, having a small land holding of 2 acres and a nuclear family. This middle class, moderately religious Jat Sikh family owns a two-room pucca house having provisions of cooking gas, electricity, television, scooter, etc. The family also owns a tractor for agricultural operations. Charanjit conceived five times and underwent 3½ months foeticide abortion thrice. At the time of survey, she had one

Case Studies 17

daughter of four years and a son of five months. She opines that in this time of dearness only two children (one male and one female) were enough as a bigger family is always faced with financial problems. Ultrasound scanning facility of prenatal sex determination was known to her from advertisements in newspapers. She believed that it was God's act that decided whether one gets a male or a female child. With a female foetus in her womb, she decided to go for female foeticide owing to the pressure of her husband, in-laws, parents and friends. She, however, had a great agony before going in for the foeticide operation. She felt guilty after getting her female foeticide operation done. She saw no good reason in meting out discrimination against the girl child in society. She rightly thinks one can provide opportunities to girl child for better education leading to her becoming a good citizen of the country and to rise to the bigger positions. She was, however, conscious that in certain homes the women giving birth to a male child get better treatment, in terms of healthier food and improved care, giving less work load as she is to rear the male child, which is considered important for the family. Therefore, this woman believes that if she were blessed with a male child she would become indifferent for the second issue. She remembers the ill treatment meted out to her by her in-laws for not giving birth to a male child. "...*jaikar kuri hoi taan paike bhaiz dewange*", she aptly remembers the words spoken to her by her in-laws before delivering the child. Thus, it is evident from this case, that female foeticide is linked to social (family preference for a male child) and economic (desire to keep family size limited due to increasing dearness) reasons. She has no regrets in going in for the foeticide operation.

In this case, respondent does not regret having undergone female foeticide thrice, perhaps bcause she ultimately got a male child.

Case 7

Raj Rani is a schedule caste Hindu woman of Nawanshahr district. This 35 years old, moderately religious housewife is educated only up to a primary level and is married for 15 years to an equally educated man of a lower middle class, schedule caste, non-agriculturist nuclear type family. The family owns two-room pucca house with facilities like cooking gas, electricity, television, bicycle, etc. This woman conceived seven times, gave stillbirth to a male child and has five living daughters of 14, 12, 11, 10 and 8 years. She also underwent a three and a half months foeticide abortion once. She got to know about the ultrasound scanning facility for sex determination from her husband. She feels that the scanning facility can be useful in planning the family size. Although she had an anxiety before going in for the foeticide operation, yet she made up her mind to go in for foeticide operation owing to the pressure of her husband and in-laws, as she had conceived a female child. Despite her large family size, she had no gender bias and ideally believed in having two children in the family. She is of the opinion that in these times of high cost of living only two children (one male and one female) were adequate as a bigger family often leads to serious hardships. She saw no good reason in meting out inequity against the girl child in society. She was, however, conscious that a mother of a male child is considered auspicious in society. Therefore, this woman believes that if she were blessed with a male child she would have become indifferent for the second issue. Her aspiration for a male child took this woman to some quacks/ sadhus, who asked her to consume some medicines with the milk of a cow who has produced a male calf, but of no use. She remembers the ill treatment meted out to her by her in-laws for not giving birth to a male child. "*...ladke nu janam na den karke khushi naal kise ne nahi bulaya na hi changi khurak diti.*" She can very well remember the condition of women after giving birth to a female child. She feels no regret in going in for the foeticide operation. Many after-effects of foeticide operation, such as, body-ache, anemia-linked weakness and difficulty in carrying out day-to-day household chores, are reported by this woman. Therefore, here, female foeticide is linked to social (family preference for a male child) and economic (desire to keep family size limited due to increasing cost of living) reasons.

A woman, having 5 daughters and 35 years old, is still trying for a male child.

Case 8

Paramjit a 28 years old woman, married for 7 years lives in Mansa district, one of the backward districts of Punjab. Both husband and wife have received primary education. They belong to Jat Sikh caste and are agriculturalists by occupation. They are economically well-off and live in a joint family. Paramjit has conceived 4 times, but has only one living

Case Studies 19

daughter. She had given birth to a son who expired shortly after birth due to some medical problem. She wants to limit her family size to two children and has been told by her husband and in-laws that son is a must for the family. Both her elder and younger brothers –in-law have a son each and this has increased the family pressure on her to bear a son. Also the tradition in the family has increased her own desire for bearing a son. According to her, a son will carry on the family name and take care of old parents. In order to give birth to a son, she has undergone two sex-selective abortions. She came to know about the advanced technology of ultrasonography to have a family of her choice through her relatives. She has been suggested to follow some superstitious beliefs by her mother-in-law to ensure the birth of a son next time. She has been prescribed some 'desi' medicine by a sadhu which is to be taken from her husband, first thing in the morning with milk of a cow that has a newly born calf. Being very religious, she considers such deeds like abortions a sin and laments the loss of her son. She says that had her son been alive, she would not have committed such a sin. Paramjit also realises that two abortions have had a detrimental effect on her health, but her desire to bear a male child is so strong, that she is willing to undergo any number of abortions till she bears her desired son.

Case 9

Kulbir, 33 is a mother of 6 daughters. The eldest is 9 years old and the youngest is 2 years old. She belongs to low caste, lives in a nuclear family. She is illiterate and her husband is a daily labourer. She is very poor and is able to meet the needs of her family with great difficulty. She knows that ultrasound is a cheap and non-invasive method of sex determination. She came to know about this technology of prenatal sex determination through her husband and relatives. She believes that this technology is helpful as one can choose the sex of the unborn child. According to her, an ideal family should have 2 sons and 1 daughter. She believes that sons are bread earners of the family and daughters will marry and go away, but son would stay and look after the family. With this mindset for having a male child, she has undergone abortion twice after sex determination test. She takes all the major decisions in the family and she herself was a willing partner to know the sex of the child and abort the foetus, if it's a female. She is of the view that girls have to be married off and that entails huge expenses on ceremonies and dowry. Her calculation is simple: better to pay a little now than to pay a huge sum later on. She feels that the first born child should be a male so that the mother can limit her family size. She does not feel sorry or considers foeticide a sin. She is willing to undergo any number of female foeticides till she gets a son and has already resorted to many superstitious means to conceive one. Though Kulbir's health has deteriorated after the abortions, her determination to have a son has not.

Case 10

Rajni Bala, an upper caste, matriculate, Khatri Hindu woman lives in Hoshiarpur district. She is a 30 years old employed lady earning a monthly Rs. 1500/-. She is married for the last 5 years to a graduate husband. She and her husband enjoy a middle class status with basic facilities such as three-room pucca house, electricity, television, radio, cooking gas, scooter, and car. She lives with her husband in a joint family having two daughters of one and four years. The family is moderately religious and visits the temple every week. Rajni Bala has been pregnant 3 times. She got her 3½ months foetus terminated, because it was a female. According to her, ideal family size is one son and one daughter. She correctly thinks that it is husband who is responsible for the sex of the foetus. She came to know about the ultrasound technology from the advertisements and is of the view that one must not go for sex determination, because in case of a female, the entire pregnancy period is full of tension and there is pressure for abortion of the female foetus. She cautions that this technology should not be misused. She agrees that there is strong male preference in the society, because sons carry family name, giving birth to a male child increases the status of the woman in the society, and mother is better looked after during her pregnancy. She says *"Is nall istari da sanmaan iskarke vadh hai kuenke usne parwaar vich vansh chaloun laee chirag ditta hai"*. She says that the male child will look after the parents in their old age. Although the male child is preferred in society, yet she thinks that it is the daughter who always thinks better of her parents. She did not go in for sex determination test in her first pregnancy. She remembers the ill treatment that she received at the hands of her family in giving birth to a female child. She says that everybody felt disappointed at the birth of female child. She recollects that some of her relatives had undergone female foeticide who now have a son. She had

Case Studies 21

consented for abortion on the advice of her in-laws because she already had two daughters and the entire family had a strong desire for a son. She is a religious lady and goes to temple every week. According to her, female foeticide is the biggest sin and deeply regrets having done it. Her health has deteriorated in terms of physical weakness. She would try for a son two more times.

Case 11

This is an interesting case of an uneducated couple of Mansa district. Forty two years old Baljinder Kaur, a Jat Sikh housewife is married for 22 years. This moderately religious family owns about 10 acres of land and a house of more than three rooms with facilities of electricity, cooking gas, television, radio etc. The family also owns a tractor for agricultural operations. Baljinder Kaur takes all important decisions in the family. She conceived eight times and has four daughters of 17, 15, 13 and 12 years. In addition, her one-month-old daughter died of jaundice. She believes that a family should have two male and one female child and that the birth of children is an act of God. Her desire for a male child took Baljinder Kaur to a Sadhu, who prescribed her some medication, gave some *Tweet* (sacred thread) and asked her to offer her services to the Gurdwara, but of no use. She learnt from her relatives, husband, neighbours and health workers about the facilities of prenatal sex determination through ultrasound technology. She believes that with this facility, the family could be kept limited. While expressing that mother gets better respect if she gives birth to a male child, Baljinder Kaur said, "*Aadmi de sir te hi ghar chalda hai.*" According to her, woman bearing a male child becomes well respected individual in the family because she has produced a 'waris' of the house and she is provided with better food and health care. Her mother-in-law felt she had burdened her husband by producing four girls. She got foetus aborted, thrice, when the pregnancies were of 3½ months. These were her unplanned pregnancies and therefore, she was not perturbed in the beginning, but felt a great regret after she knew that she was carrying female child. After the foeticide operation, she felt physical weakness. The main reason for foeticide was their already having four daughters in the family. Due to this, her husband and in-laws approved of her going in for female foeticide operations. She had some nervousness and anxiety before the foeticide operation. She says that none of her relatives had ever gone for a foeticide operation. She felt that female foeticide is a great sin. The pressing family circumstances forced her to commit this sin.

Case 12

Sylvia Smith, 23 years old, a housewife belonging to Christian community living in a village of Ferozepur district, is married to an illiterate man belonging to a family owning a pucca house with all facilities of electricity, cooking gas, bicycle, and radio etc. This moderately religious lady lives with her husband and two daughters of three and one years. She attends the Church every week. Sylvia Smith has been pregnant 4 times. Once she got her foetus aborted because it was a female and once she had a miscarriage. She believed that an ideal family size is having one son and one daughter. She believes that the sex of the child depends on the will of the God. She is aware of the ultrasound scanning facilities for the determination of sex of the unborn baby which she learnt from her relatives. She feels that going in for sex determination is a fine thing. In this context she says *"Jaikar pata lag jaye ke munda hai taan man khush hunda hai ke saade ghar da waris aa gaya hai."* She agrees that there is strong male preference in the society because sons are considered to carry the family name forward. Giving birth to a male child increases the status of the women in the society, and the mother is often better looked after. Sylvia Smith feels that the first issue should be male and expresses *"Munda howe taan fikar mitt janda hai te dusri kudi howe taan koi gal nahin ke saade parivaar nu vadaon vala aa gaya hai."* She underwent the 3½ months female foeticide operations, both under her own motivation, and that of her husband. She went for this because she did not want to add any more daughters to her family that already had two daughters. She was nervous before going in for this operation. She discloses that some of her relatives also underwent female foeticide. She thinks that if she does not get the male child, she would go in for conception four more times.

Case 13

Jagmohan Kaur, a Jat Sikh woman lives in Ballianwal village of Bathinda district. She is a 30 years old housewife married for last 5 years. Both she and her husband are matriculate. The family owns more than 15 acres of land and enjoys living facilities such as a three room pucca house with radio, television, bicycle and scooter. The family also owns a tractor for agricultural purposes. She lives in a joint family with

Case Studies 23

her husband and a daughter of two years. She cannot take important decisions in their day to day family life. Jagmohan Kaur has a religious background as she visited Gurudwara every week. She conceived thrice. She believed that a family should have one male and one female child and that the birth of children is in the control of the God. She learnt from newspaper advertisements, her relatives and husband about the facilities of prenatal sex determination through ultrasound tests. She believed that through sex determination, the family could be kept limited. This is useful in getting rid of the birth of a female child and thus avoid the unnecessary burden on the family. While expressing that the mother gets better respect if she gives birth to a male child, Jagmohan Kaur said, *"Kuenke puttar nu hi ghar da waris samjaya janda hai. Kudi de muqable munde nu parivaar ate samaj vich ucha sthan prapat hai."* According to her, people paid more care to a woman who gives birth to a male child and she is even pampered for it. She says *"Puttar nu janam dain wali istari nu changa samjaya janda hai. Kudi de janam nu pathar keha janda hai. Munde di tandrusti laee maan da ve jayada khayal rakhya janda hai."* She believed that if the first issue in the family is male, there remains no longing for a male child any more, in this way there is no need of going in for subsequent foeticide abortion and the lady gets a respectable place in the family. Jagmohan Kaur did not think of getting the foetal sex determination during her first pregnancy. Although she was not meted out shabby treatment when she delivered a female child, nevertheless there was no celebration or delight either. "The relatives and acquaintances visiting me expressed their condolences for the birth of the female child that generated a sort of inferiority complex in me", says Jagmohan Kaur. Her desire for the male child took her to different places suggested by others, but nothing could work. With pressure from her in-laws, parents, friends and husband, she made her mind to go in for female foeticide abortion. She got her foetus aborted at four months pregnancy. She takes responsibility for this decision on herself, as there is a discrimination against the girl child in society. It is difficult to send the girl outside for education and other activities. There is problem of dowry while marrying her off. Unlike her male counterpart, a female is subjected to various apprehensions for tarnishing the familiy's image. The woman giving birth to female children is looked upon with disgrace in the society. She is even referred to as a 'kulhini' in the society out of malice. Although this was her unplanned pregnancy, yet she was perturbed and nervous before going in for foeticide abortion. She felt a great regret after she knew that she was carrying a female child. After the foeticide operation, she felt physical weakness and was shocked for having committed this sin. According to Jagmohan Kaur, there is a tremendous pressure of society and one has to go according to it. The main reason for this foeticide was social. She remembers that some of her relatives had also gone for foeticide operation. She would try to get a male issue twice, but to maintain family size, she would not hesitate going in for an abortion if the fetous is female.

Case 14

Maya is a 32 years old low caste, Hindu woman married for 14 years. She lives in a village in Fatehgarh Sahib district which has lowest sex ratio in Punjab. She has 3 children - one son aged 8 years and two daughters aged 6 and 2 years respectively. Subsequently, she has aborted female foetus twice, as according to her, an ideal family should have two sons. She and her husband are both illiterate and of low socio-economic status. Her family lives in a rented one room *kucha* house. She became aware of the sex determination tests through her relatives. Maya is of the view that the first child should always be a male as it increases the respect of the mother in her in-laws' house. She never went in for sex-determination tests in her first three pregnancies as her financial condition does not permit her to get these tests done and pay for abortions. Now she desperately wants to give birth to another son as according to her – *Ik aankh da koi maan nahin is layee dooji aankh honi jaroori hai*. One son is a cause for joy but two sons are seen as a lifetime celebration, the traditional thinking being if something happens to one, at least the other will take care of the parents. She, therefore, borrowed money from her relatives to undergo two selective abortions. She thinks that society is biased towards males and giving birth to one more son would increase her status in her in-laws family and also guarantee her more social security in old age. She herself wanted to undergo sex-determination tests and then decided for abortions. Her other relatives have also undergone similar abortions. She feels guilty for having committed this sin of female foeticide twice. It has also lead to deterioration in her health and has also been a financial strain on the family but she wants to have 'a jodi' of sons.

Thus it depicts that the social desire for sons have trapped women in the never-ending bind for a male-child at any cost.

Case 15

Ramnita is a young woman of 21 years married for 10 months. She belongs to upper caste Jat Sikh family. She is a matriculate and her husband is a graduate. They are big farmers and own car and tractors. She is a housewife and lives in a joint family. Ramnita is very religious and visits gurudwara everyday. She believes in a very small family and according to her ideal number of children in the family are only one son and no daughter. She is one of the rare ones who went for sex determination even during her first pregnancy and subsequently got it aborted because it was a female. She came to know about ultrasound technology for sex determination through advertisements. She believes, it is better to know the sex of the foetus because one can avoid having a daughter. Reasons that she gave for not having a daughter are dowry, expenditure on education, social insecurity for girls, in general escalating cost of living. According to her, if daughter does something wrong, the whole family gets a bad name, but if son goes wrong then society does not say anything. She is of the view that daughters are meant to be married to another family and she does not want son-in-law to inherit their land. She feels that there is preference to a male child in the society and that woman who gives birth to a male child is looked after very well by her in-laws. Though she is a lady of very firm views, still her level of decision making in the family is very low. She cannot even decide what to cook. She never went to any saint or mahatma for a son. She went for female foeticide willingly on the advice of her husband, parents and mother-in-law. She does not regret having undergone female foeticide and she plans to repeat the same during next pregnancy and would try any number of times for a male child. Though she is a very religious lady, who visits gurudwara daily, but still says that female foeticide is not a sin.

It is unfortunate that some one, who is educated, and very religious is so insensitive and heartless when it comes to female foeticide.

4
Analysis

In most of the studies on such social issues, only subjective analysis is done. The reason is that firstly, data collected is not exhaustive and secondly, case histories are very few.

In the present study, each respondent was asked 40 questions and total number of selected case histories is 374. Social problems, such as gender bias or female foeticide, are multidimensional. Our thinking and perceptions are built over generations, which are interplay of various social, cultural, historical and economic factors. I decided to look at this problem objectively, for which quantitative analysis was a must. This was necessary to understand how various factors influence the psyche of the women. For example, one must see objectively the difference in perception of an illiterate and an educated woman, regarding preference to male child in our society.

Now, to enable objective analysis, it was necessary to quantify the data. The subjective responses were classified into discrete categories and the data was fed into the computer for analysis. Later on, statistical test was applied to see how various socio-economic factors such as education, caste, religion, financial status, religious status affect perception and thinking of women who have undergone female foeticide.

4.1 Computerisation of the Data

The data recorded in 374 case histories was classified into discrete categories to enable quantitative analysis. For example; in question on financial status, the respondent was asked about the assets owned by the family and based on that her financial status was classified as

a) *high:-* who possessed land+pucca house+car/tractor;
b) *middle:-* land up to 2 acre+pucca house+scooter;
c) *poor:-* no land+kucha house.

Analysis 27

Similarly in cases of subjective response such as Q 20 - why preference is given to the boys? Response was classified into eight categories—for carrying family name, look after in old age, enhanced respect in the society, contribution to the economy of the family, girls as financial liability.

For analysis, a team of computer engineer and doctors of the Punjab Health Systems Corporation (PHSC) developed software in Oracle. Front End Forms are in Developer 2000 and Back End in Oracle 8i. The data was fed by seven computer operators, and was 100% cross-checked.

A filled up questionnaire in Punjabi language is at Annexure – I. It's English translation is at Annexure – II. Front End Forms for feeding data into the computer is at Annexure -III

4.2 Results and Observations

Table-1 (Q-1) : No. of case histories received district wise.

Sr.No	Name of Distt.	No. of case histories
1	Amritsar	66
2	Bathinda	23
3	Fatehgarh Sahib	11
4	Faridkot	27
5	Ferozepur	15
6	Gurdaspur	6
7	Hoshiarpur	45
8	Jalandhar	18
9	Kapurthala	3
10	Ludhiana	5
11	Mansa	42
12	Moga	15
13	Mukatsar	6
14	Nawanshahr	24
15	Patiala	19
16	Ropar	35
17	Sangrur	14
Total		374

Out of the 500 forms distributed to Istri Sehat Sabha members, only 374 could be included in the study, rest were rejected due to incomplete information.

Table-2 (Q2) : Age distribution of respondents.

Age Group (Yrs.)	No. of Respondents	Percentage (%)
<20	1	0.3
20-25	65	17.3
26-30	192	51.3
31-35	84	22.5
>35	32	8.6

About 92% respondents were in the age group of 20 to 35 years. Still a large number of them - 8% were more than 35 years of age.

Table-3 (Q3) : Duration of married life.

No. of Years	No. of Respondents	Percentage (%)
<2	2	0.5
3-5	83	22.2
6-10	175	46.8
11-15	73	19.5
16-20	37	9.9
>20	4	1.1

69% of respondents were married for 3-10 years (N=248), interestingly 4 respondents were married for over 20 yrs. Very few (.5%) were married for less than 2 years, this is because at the time of first pregnancy, rarely any one went for sex determination.

Table-4 (Q4) : Educational status of respondents.

Edu. Status	No. of Respondents	Percentage (%)
Illiterate	71	19.0
Educated	276	74.0
Highly Educated	26	7.0

Repondents were categorised as educated if they had formal education upto class 12. Those possesing graduation qualification and above were included in highly educated status. Very few women (7%) are graduates.

Analysis

Table-5 (Q5) : Employment status of respondents.

Employed	No. of Respondents	Percentage (%)
No	341	91.9
Yes	30	8.1

Majority of respondents were home makers. Only 8% were gainfully employed.

Table-6 (Q6) : Educational status of husband.

Edu. Status	No. of Respondents	Percentage (%)
Illiterate	52	13.9
Educated	285	76.4
Highly Educated	36	9.7

Table 4 and 6 depict the educational status of respondents and their spouses. Majority belongs to educated group, that is upto class 12.

Table-7 (Q7) : Economic status of respondents

Economic Status	No. of Respondents	Percentage (%)
High	32	8.6
Middle	295	78.9
Poor	47	12.5

Economic status was classified as (a) High: who possesed land+pucca house+car/ tractor (b) Middle: land upto 2 acre+pucca house+scooter. (c) Poor: no land+kucha house. Majority of them were from middle income group.

Table-8 (Q8) : Caste division.

Caste	No. of Respondents	Percentage (%)
Lower	148	40.4
Upper	218	59.6

Respondents were well distributed between upper and lower caste. Upper caste had 59.5% (N=218) of respondents against lower caste 40.4% (N=148). Scheduled castes were classified as lower caste. Backward castes and higher castes were classified as upper caste. Some of them did not mention their caste (N=8).

Table-9 (Q9) : Religion of respondents.

Religion	No. of Respondents	Percentage (%)
Sikh	230	61.4
Hindu	142	38.0
Muslim	1	0.3
Christian	1	0.3

61.4% were Sikhs, 38% were Hindus. This bias may be on account of demographic pattern.

Table-10 (Q10) : Joint families.

Joint Family	No. of Respondents	Percentage (%)
Yes	207	55.8
No	164	44.2

Majority of respondents 207 (56%) were from joint families. This may be due to the fact that they were from rural and semi-urban areas.

Table-11 (Q11) : Religious status of respondents.

Religious Status	No. of Respondents	Percentage (%)
Very Religious	114	30.6
Religious	224	60.1
Not Religious	35	9.3

Religious status was derived according to number of times the respondents visited the place of worship. Those who visited once in a while were termed as religious and regular visitors were termed as very religious. Very few (9.3%) are not religious, that is they don't visit the place of worship.

Table-12 (Q12-A) : Cases as per total no. of children.

Total Children	No. of Respondents	Percentage (%)
1	76	20.5
2	153	41.4
3	91	24.6
4	29	7.8
5	17	4.6
>5	4	1.1

62% (N=229) respondents had 1 or 2 living children. Very few, 14% had 4 or more children. Majority is from small family.

Analysis

Table-13 (Q12-B) : Cases as per total no. of male children.

Male children	No. of Respondents	Percentage (%)
0	225	61.6
1	125	34.3
2	15	4.1

62% (N=225) respondents at the time of interview did not have a male child. 38% either subsequently got a male child, that is, were succesful in their objective or wanted to have two male children.

Table-14 (Q12-C) :Cases as per total no. of female children.

Female children	No. of Respondents	Percentage (%)
0	8	2.2
1	132	35.6
2	140	37.7
3	65	17.5
4	19	5.1
>4	7	1.9

Vast majority of respondents (73%) opted for foeticide when they had 1/2 living female children. However 2.2% (N=8) also opted for foeticide when they had no living female child. 98% respondents were not against female child, but wanted to have atleast one male child.

Table-15 (Q12-D) : Age group of respondents at first birth.

Age(Yrs.)	No. of Respondents	Percentage (%)
<20	48	14.4
20-25	240	71.9
26-30	42	12.6
>30	4	1.1

72% Respondents were in the age group of 20 to 25 when they had their first baby. Significantly 14.2% of study population attained motherhood at less than 20 years.

Table-16 (Q12-E) : Age group of respodents when first male child was born.

Age(Yrs.)	No. of Respondents	Percentage (%)
<20	4	3.1
20-25	50	39.1
26-30	54	42.2
>30	20	15.6

81% of the respondents had their first male child between age 20-30 years 15.6% had their first male child after 30 years, which is significantly higher than 1.2% of >30 years at the time of first child.

Table-17 (Q12-F) : Cases as per no. of children after male child birth.

No. of Children	No. of Respondents	Percentage (%)
0	163	79.1
1	25	12.1
2	15	7.3
>2	3	1.5

Subsequent births after the male child was born in the family was very low. This shows that vast majority (79%) are particular about small family.

Table-18 (Q13) : Cases as per no. of pregnancies in respondents.

No. of Pregnancies	No. of Respondents	Percentage (%)
1	1	0.3
2	53	14.2
3	115	30.9
4	99	26.6
5	53	14.2
6	33	8.9
7	11	3.0
>7	7	1.9

45 % (N=148) had 2-3 pregnancies whereas 28% mothers had atleast 5 pregnancies. It is important to note that 14.2% (N=53) opted for female foeticide when they just had 2 pregnancies.

Analysis 33

Table-19 (Q15-A) : Desired no. of male children by respondent.

Desired No. of Males	No. of Respondents	Percentage (%)
0	-	-
1	250	67.6
2	116	31.3
>2	4	1.1

Majority 67.6% (N=250) had a desire to have one male baby, that means small family. 31.4% of them wished to have 2 male children.

Table-20 (Q15-B) : Desired no. of female children by respondent.

Desired No. of Females	No. of Respondents	Percentage (%)
0	12	3.3
1	318	86.6
2	32	8.7
>2	5	1.4

Maximum No. 86.6% (N=318) wished to have one female child only. Very few (3.3%) do not desire any female child. This shows that women are not against having daughters.

Table-21 (Q16) : Expressed opinion regarding who is responsible for sex of the child.

Opinion	No. of Respondents	Percentage (%)
God	261	70.0
Husband	107	28.7
Wife	5	1.3

70% of respondents held God responsible for sex of the child. 28.7% of respondents answered correctly that husband was responsible for the sex of newborn.

Table-22 (Q17) : Awareness about prenatal testing for sex selection.

Prior Knowledge	No. of Respondents	Percentage (%)
Yes	311	83.8
No	60	16.2

There is universal awarness about sex determination as related by the data. 83.8% (N=311) had prior knowledge about it.

Table-23 (Q18) : Source of information about prenatal testing.

Source of information	No. of Respondents	Percentage(%)
Advertisement	98	26.7
Husband	65	17.7
Family member	49	13.3
Health Worker	34	9.3
Others	121	33.0

Major source of information was through advertisements (26.7%). However 33% of respondents could not identify the source of knowledge.

Table-24 (Q19-A) : Should mother know sex of unborn child.

Opinion	No. of Respondents	Percentage (%)
Yes	232	62.0
No	142	38.0

Table-25 (Q19-B) : Why mother should not know sex of unborn child.

Reasons	No. of Respondents	Percentage (%)
Antenatal period will be full of tension if unborn is female	23	39.7
Pressure from others to abort female foetus	18	31.0

Table-26 (Q19-C): Why mother should know sex of unborn child.

Reasons	No. of Respondents	Percentage (%)
Choose the sex according to needs/desire	67	47.2
Antenatal care if unborn is male	12	8.5
Limit Family size	59	41.5
Respect increases in society/in-laws	4	2.8

Majority of respondents 62% (N=232) were of the opinion that the mother should know the sex of unborn child. Amongst those who were against this, large number cited (39.7%) that this information will increase the tension during period of pregnancy if unborn is a female child. Those who favoured to know the sex felt that one could select/choose the sex according to desire/need. 41.5% (N=59) felt the information can be used as a Family Planning Measure.

Analysis

Table-27 (Q20-A): Whether preference is given to boys in society.

Response	No. of Respondents	Percentage (%)
Yes	335	89.8
No	38	10.2

Table-28 (Q20-B) : Whether preference given to boys is justified

Response	No. of Respondents	Percentage (%)
Right	150	40.2
Wrong	223	59.8

Table-29 (Q20-C) : Reasons for preference given to boys.

Reasons	No. of Respondents	Percentage (%)
For carrying family name	60	35.7
Look after in old age	35	20.8
Enhanced respect in society	27	16.1
Contributing to economy of family	21	12.5
Social compulsion	14	8.3
Looking after family inheritance	4	2.4
Girls are financial liability	5	3.0
Girls go away after marriage	2	1.2

90% agreed that boys are preferred in society. However, only 40% felt that this social attitude was justified. Various reasons have been cited for giving preference to the boys in society. 35.7% thought that boys were preferred because they carry family name. 20.8% felt that boys are needed for looking after in old age. Very few gave financial reasons.

Table-30 (Q21) : Perception of respondents about status of women who had a son.

Enhanced status	No. of Respondents	Percentage (%)
Yes	338	90.6
No	35	9.4

90.6% felt that having a male child enhanced the women's status in society.

Table-31 (Q22): Perceptions regarding improved post natal care.

Post natal care improved	No. of Respondents	Percentage (%)
Yes	312	84.3
No	58	15.7

84.3% of respondents had the perception that post natal care of the mother was much better after male child birth.

Table-32 (Q23) : The level of decision making in the household.

Level	No. of Respondents	Percentage (%)
High	121	32.9
Medium	92	25.0
Low	155	42.1

Level of decision making in the household was decided from 5 different questions asked to the respondents from the questionaire. If the respondent had the right to decide as to when she should bear a child, she was categorised under high level. If she gave affirmative answer to even one question asked, she was placed under medium level. 42.1% had low level of decision making in household whereas 32.9% reported high level of decision making.

Table-33 (Q24-A) : Opinion regarding the sex of first child.

Opinion	No. of Respondents	Percentage (%)
Male	207	55.9
Female	15	4.1
Any	148	40.0

55.9% felt that first child should be male. Whereas 40% felt it could be any.

Analysis

Table-34 (Q24-B) : Reasons given for the preferred sex.

Reasons	No. of Respondents	Percentage (%)
Boys:		
Boys are needed in the family	40	19.8
It relieves from the worries about the sex of next child	115	56.9
Enhance status of women	22	10.9
Any:		
Health of child is main consideration	15	7.4
Can go in for sex determination test second time	10	5.0

Major reasons given for preferred sex were that it relieved the mother from the worries about the sex of the subsequent child.

Table-35 (Q25) : Whether respondents opted for sex determination during 1st pregnancy.

Response	No. of Respondents	Percentage (%)
No	319	86.0
Yes	52	14.0

86% did not opt for sex determination during first pregnancy.

Table-36 (Q26-A) : Any maltreatment meted out to respondents for not having a male child.

Response	No. of Respondents	Percentage (%)
Yes	85	23.1
No	284	76.9

Table-37 (Q26-B) : Mode of maltreatment.

Maltreatment	No. of Respondents	Percentage(%)
Mental torture	58	82.9
Physical abuse	7	10.0
Threat of second marriage of Husband	2	2.9
Forced abortions	3	4.2

76.9% did not report any maltreatment. Of the 23.1% respondents who reported maltreatment following female child birth, 82.9% were given mental torture and 10% were physically abused.

Table-38 (Q27) : Beliefs in superstitions to get a male child.

Response	No. of Respondents	Percentage (%)
Yes	165	44.5
No	206	55.5

55.5% did not believe in any superstitions to fulfill their desire to have a male child.

Table-39 (Q28-A) : No. of induced abortions.

No. of induced abortions	No. of Respondents	Percentage (%)
1	304	81.5
2	54	14.5
3	11	2.9
4	3	0.8
>4	1	0.3

1 Induced abortion was reported by 81.5% (N=304) as against this 14.5% had 2 induced abortions. 1 case reported more then 4 induced abortions.

Table-40 (Q28-C) : No. of female children at the time of abortion.

No. of living female child	No. of Respondents	Percentage (%)
0	7	1.9
1	144	38.6
2	143	38.3
3	59	15.8
>3	20	5.4

More than 76% (N=287) of respondents had 1/2 living female children when they opted for induced abortion. Only 1.9% did not have a female child when they went for abortion. This shows vast majority (98%) are not against daughters.

Table-41 (Q30) : Feelings experienced by respondents before USG.

Feelings	No. of Respondents	Percentage (%)
Normal	45	12.4
Worried	258	70.9
Apprehensive	61	16.7

Majority (70.9%) were worried about the sex of child before USG.

Analysis 39

Table-42 (Q31): Feelings experienced by respondents when they were informed about the female foetus after USG.

Feelings	No. of Respondents	Percentage (%)
Normal	17	4.8
Sad	119	33.3
Tense	221	61.9

61.9% (N=221) reported tension after learning the USG result that baby was female. Less than 5% were normal.

Table-43 (Q32) : Reasons for Female Foeticide.

Reasons	No. of Respondents	Percentage (%)
Previous 1/2/3/4 daughters	235	71.1
To give birth to 1/2 sons	53	16.0
Financial Reasons	20	6.0
Limit family size	15	4.5
Girls not considered at par	8	2.4

235 respondents (71.1%) went in for female foeticide because they previously had daughters, and now wanted a male child. Surprisingly only 6% gave financial reasons such as dowry.

Table-44 (Q33) : Who suggested to undergo abortion.

Suggested by	No. of Respondents	Percentage (%)
Family	127	34.1
Husband	153	41.1
Self	92	24.7

In majority of cases (41.1%) husband had suggested to go in for foeticide. In 24.7% cases, respondent herself wished to undergo foeticide.

Table-45 (Q35): Whether any relative underwent Female Foeticide.

Abortion amongst relatives	No. of Respondents	Percentage (%)
No	274	77.0
Yes	82	23.0

Relatives of 23% of respondents underwent female foeticide.

Table-46 (Q36) : Feeling of regret after Female Foeticide.

Regret feeling	No. of Respondents	Percentage (%)
No	138	37.0
Yes	235	63.0

63% regretted their action of undergoing foeticide.

Table-47 (Q37-A) : Whether it is a sin to commit Female Foeticide.

Opinion	No. of Respondents	Percentage (%)
No	60	16.1
Yes	313	83.9
Large number of them (84%) already had the realisation that foeticide was a sin.		

Table-48 (Q37-B) : Whether Respondents would repeat Female Foeticide

Repeat Female foeticide	No. of Respondents	Percentage (%)
No	262	70.2
Yes	111	29.7

Table-49 (Q37-C) : Reasons to repeat Female Foeticide.

Reasons	No. of Respondents	Percentage (%)
To give birth to 1/2 sons	48	52.7
Desire to limit family	15	16.5
Economic reasons	15	16.5
Previous 1/2/3 daughters	13	14.3
70% said that they would not repeat the act of foeticide. Majority who said that they would repeat, wanted to have a male child.		

Table-50 (Q40) : No. of tries for getting a male child.

No. of tries	No. of Respondents	Percentage (%)
0	13	4.5
1	44	15.2
2-3	176	60.7
4	36	12.4
>4	21	7.2
19.6% respondents were willing to give 4 or more tries in case they don't bear a male child. This shows how strong the desire is to have a male child.		

Analysis

5. Preference to male child. This explains the perception of the lady with regard to gender bias in our society.
6. Whether preference to male child is right or wrong. This explains the feelings of the lady towards gender bias prevalent in the society, whether, according to her, it is justified or not.
7. Consent for abortion. This explains whether the lady was willing for abortion or she was pressurised and forced by her family members.
8. Sin to kill female foetus.
9. Regret after abortion. That is, whether the respondent regrets having undergone female foeticide.
10. Repeat abortion. That is, whether the respondent is planning to repeat female foeticide in case she does not conceive a male child.
11. Number of tries for male child. This shows level of desperation in the respondent and her family for male child.
12. What is more relevant - caste or religion.

Symbols used in the analysis

(i) α = level of significance. α is taken as .05. This means the conclusions drawn would be 95% times correct.
(ii) χ^2 = Value of Chi-Square. If this value is less than the critical value, then the categories do not affect a particular response. If value of Chi-Square is more than the critical value, then the categories do have an impact on that particular response.

Table I : Age At Marriage					
Categories	No. of Respondents	<18 Yrs	18-21 Yrs	>=22 Yrs	Chi-Square Test
Caste:					
Lower	148	18 (12.2%)	97 (65.5%)	33 (22.3%)	$\chi^2 = 2.33$
Upper	218	26 (12.0%)	128 (58.7%)	64 (29.4%)	Insignificant
Education:					
Illiterate	71	12 (17.0%)	45 (63.4%)	14 (19.7%)	$\chi^2 = 3.51$
Educated	302	32 (10.6%)	185 (61.3%)	85 (28.1%)	Insignificant
Religion:					
Sikh	230	24 (10.4%)	146 (63.5%)	60 (26.1%)	$\chi^2 = 1.41$
Hindu	142	20 (14.1%)	83 (58.5%)	39 (27.5%)	Insignificant

Observations

- For women, minimum legally permissible age for marriage is 18 years. Since respondents were from rural and semi urban areas of Punjab, it is expected that age at marriage would be on the lower side. 63% of the respondents married between the age of 18-21 years. Still a large number of them (12%), were married when they were less than 18 years old, which is surprising because Punjab is a progressive state and one expects that girls are not married below 18 years.

- Common belief is that girls of families belonging to lower strata of the society are married early. The value of Chi-Square for all categories of caste, religion, education is less than the corresponding critical values, which means that the difference in the percentages for all categories is due to chance alone and that all these categories such as lower and upper caste, illiterate and educated, Hindu and Sikh do not have significant impact on age at marriage. Religion has the least impact on age at the time of marriage. Hindus and Sikhs marry their daughters alike.

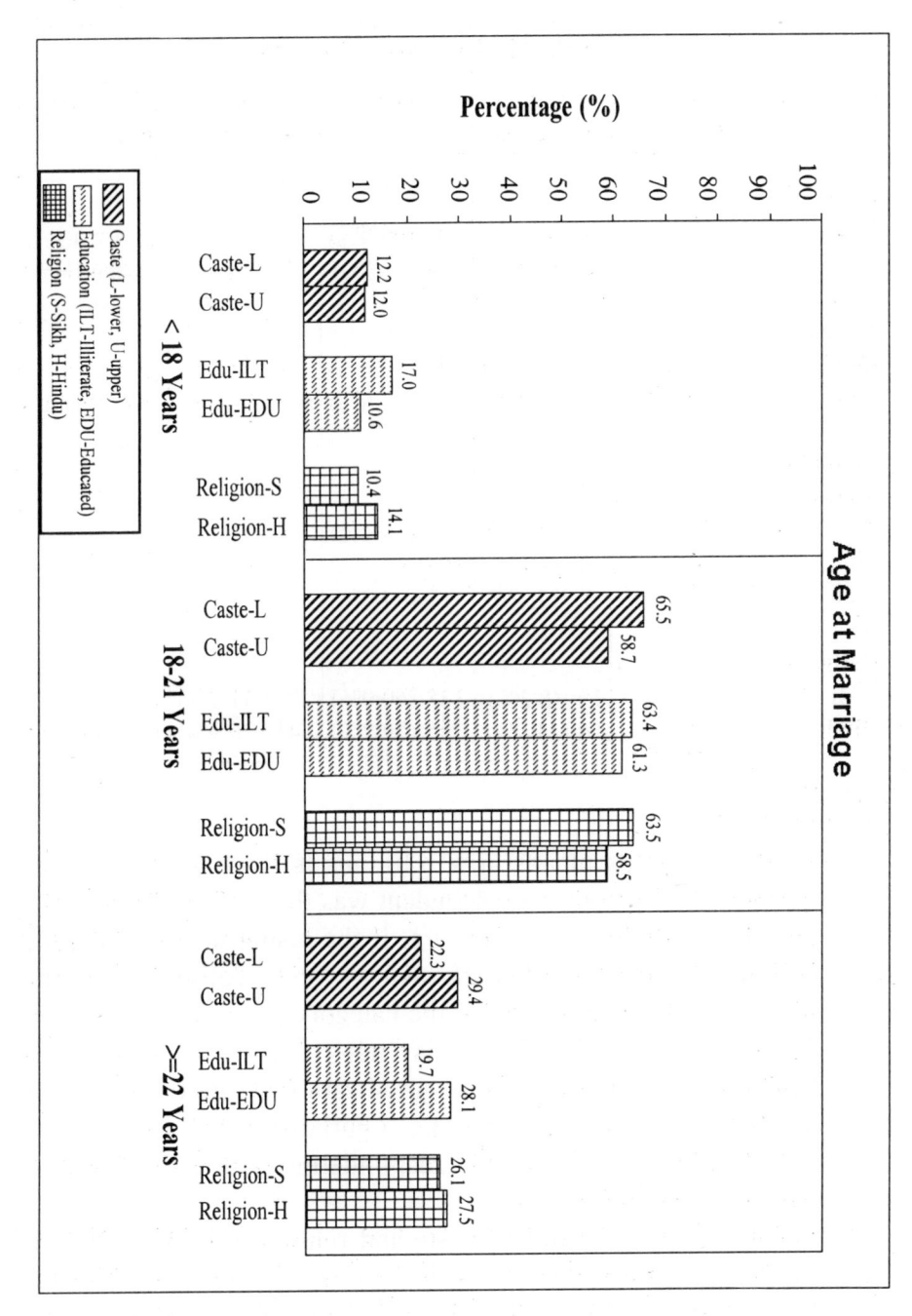

Analysis

Age at Marriage

< 18 Years
- Caste-L: 12.2
- Caste-U: 12.0
- Edu-ILT: 17.0
- Edu-EDU: 10.6
- Religion-S: 10.4
- Religion-H: 14.1

18-21 Years
- Caste-L: 65.5
- Caste-U: 58.7
- Edu-ILT: 63.4
- Edu-EDU: 61.3
- Religion-S: 63.5
- Religion-H: 58.5

>=22 Years
- Caste-L: 22.3
- Caste-U: 29.4
- Edu-ILT: 19.7
- Edu-EDU: 28.1
- Religion-S: 26.1
- Religion-H: 27.5

Legend:
- Caste (L-lower, U-upper)
- Education (ILT-Illiterate, EDU-Educated)
- Religion (S-Sikh, H-Hindu)

Table II: Religious Status

Categories	No. of Respondents	Not Religious	Religious	Very Religious	Chi-Square Test
Caste:					
Lower	148	16 (10.8%)	96 (64.9%)	36 (24.3%)	$\chi^2 = 4.40$
Upper	218	18 (8.3%)	125 (57.3%)	75 (34.4%)	Insignificant
Education:					
Illiterate	71	14 (19.7%)	49 (69.0%)	8 (11.3%)	$\chi^2 = 19.91$
Educated	302	24 (7.9%)	172 (57.0%)	106 (35.1%)	Significant
Financial Status:					
Poor	47	9 (19.1%)	28 (59.6%)	10 (21.3%)	$\chi^2 = 17.43$
Middle	295	24 (8.1%)	185 (62.7%)	86 (29.2%)	Significant
Rich	32	3 (9.4%)	11 (34.3%)	18 (56.3%)	
Religion:					
Sikh	230	19 (8.3%)	138 (60.0%)	73 (31.7%)	$\chi^2 = 1.08$
Hindu	142	16 (11.2%)	85 (59.9%)	41 (28.9%)	Insignificant

Observations

- Religious Status means how religious is the respondent. The question asked from the respondent was that how frequently she goes to a temple or a gurudwara. If the response was daily, the respondent has been categorised as "very religious", if the response was once in a week the category is "religious" and for other response the category is "not religious". Most of the respondents visited temple or gurudwara once in a while. Only less than 10% did not visit temple or gurudwara, that is, they were "not religious". 30% of the respondents visited the place of worship once in a week.
- For different categories of caste and religion the value of Chi-Square ($\chi 2$) is less than the critical value, which means caste and religion do not affect religiosity of the women. Lower and upper caste, Sikh and Hindu equally believe in God.
- Education and financial status of the respondent do have an impact on the religious status of the respondent. Educated women

Analysis

are more religious in the sense that they visit gurudwara or temple more frequently. 35% of educated women visited the place of worship daily as against 11% of the illiterate women. The reason may be that illiterate women belong to poor families and quite a large number of them are daily wage earners and thus get less time to visit temple or gurudwara. Similarly, women of rich families visited temple or gurudwara much more frequently than their counterparts. 50% women of rich families, 29% of middle class and 21% of poor visited the place of worship daily. Here again reason may be the same, women belonging to rich families have more time and means to visit place of worship.

Female Foeticide: Myth and Reality

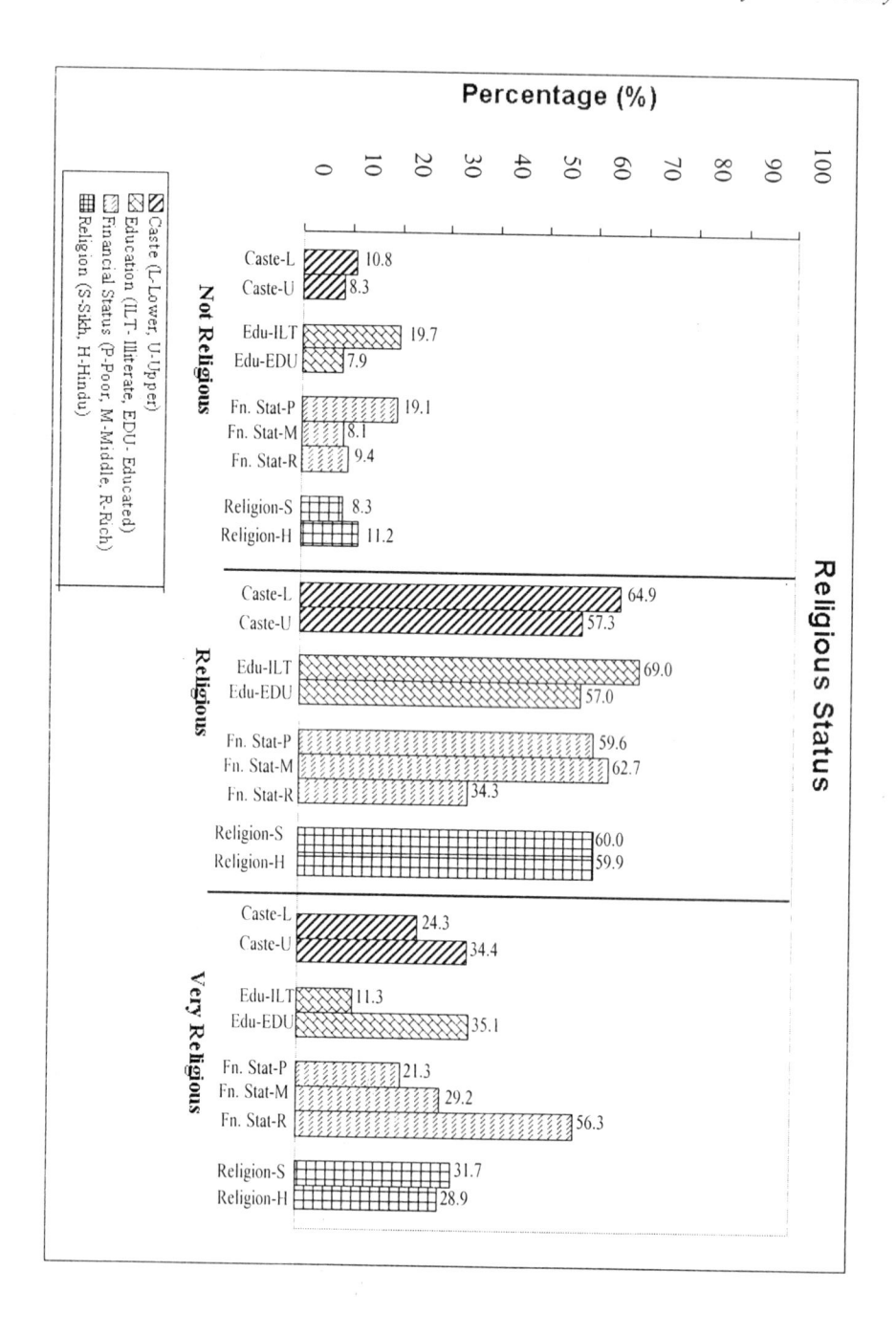

Chart: Religious Status

Legend:
- Caste (L-Lower, U-Upper)
- Education (ILT- Illiterate, EDU- Educated)
- Financial Status (P-Poor, M-Middle, R-Rich)
- Religion (S-Sikh, H-Hindu)

Not Religious
Category	Percentage (%)
Caste-L	10.8
Caste-U	8.3
Edu-ILT	19.7
Edu-EDU	7.9
Fn. Stat-P	19.1
Fn. Stat-M	8.1
Fn. Stat-R	9.4
Religion-S	8.3
Religion-H	11.2

Religious
Category	Percentage (%)
Caste-L	64.9
Caste-U	57.3
Edu-ILT	69.0
Edu-EDU	57.0
Fn. Stat-P	59.6
Fn. Stat-M	62.7
Fn. Stat-R	34.3
Religion-S	60.0
Religion-H	59.9

Very Religious
Category	Percentage (%)
Caste-L	24.3
Caste-U	34.4
Edu-ILT	11.3
Edu-EDU	35.1
Fn. Stat-P	21.3
Fn. Stat-M	29.2
Fn. Stat-R	56.3
Religion-S	31.7
Religion-H	28.9

Analysis

Table III: Ideal Family Size (Desired No. of Children)

Categories	No. of Respondent	M=1, F=1*	M=2, F=1	Others	Chi-Square Test
Caste:					
Lower	148	75 (50.7%)	42 (28.4%)	31 (20.9%)	$\chi^2 = 9.01$ Significant
Upper	218	144 (66.1%)	46 (21.1%)	28 (12.8%)	
Education:					
Illiterate	71	28 (39.4%)	23 (32.4%)	20 (28.1%)	$\chi^2 = 16.84$ Significant
Educated	302	196 (65.0%)	66 (21.9%)	40 (13.2%)	
Financial Status:					
Poor	47	19 (40.4%)	16 (34.0%)	12 (25.5%)	$\chi^2 = 14.08$ Significant
Middle	295	181 (61.4%)	71 (24.1%)	43 (14.6%)	
Rich	32	25 (78.1%)	2 (6.3%)	5 (15.6%)	
Religion:					
Sikh	230	144 (62.6%)	48 (20.9%)	38 (16.5%)	$\chi^2 = 3.09$ Insignificant
Hindu	142	80 (56.3%)	41 (28.9%)	21 (14.8%)	

* M = Male Child, F = Female Child

Observations

- Respondents were asked, what according to them was the ideal number of sons and daughters in a family. The most important thing to be noticed is, that hardly any one desired only sons and no daughter, which means they were not against the girl child. According to most of them (60%) ideal family consisted of one son and one daughter, 26% desired two sons and one daughter. The second category mostly belonged to lower strata of the society, who wanted to be doubly sure for the male child.
- For religion, the value of Chi-Square is less than the critical value, which means Hindu and Sikh desire the number of children alike.
- Caste, education and financial status of the family, significantly affect the desired number of children. More number of upper caste families desired one son and one daughter, whereas greater percentage of lower castes desired two sons and one daughter. One son and one daughter were desired by 65% of the educated respondents against 39% of illiterate respondents. Similarly, 78% of the rich wanted one son and one daughter whereas poor respondents wanted more number of children. This shows that upper strata of the society are more particular about smaller size of the family.

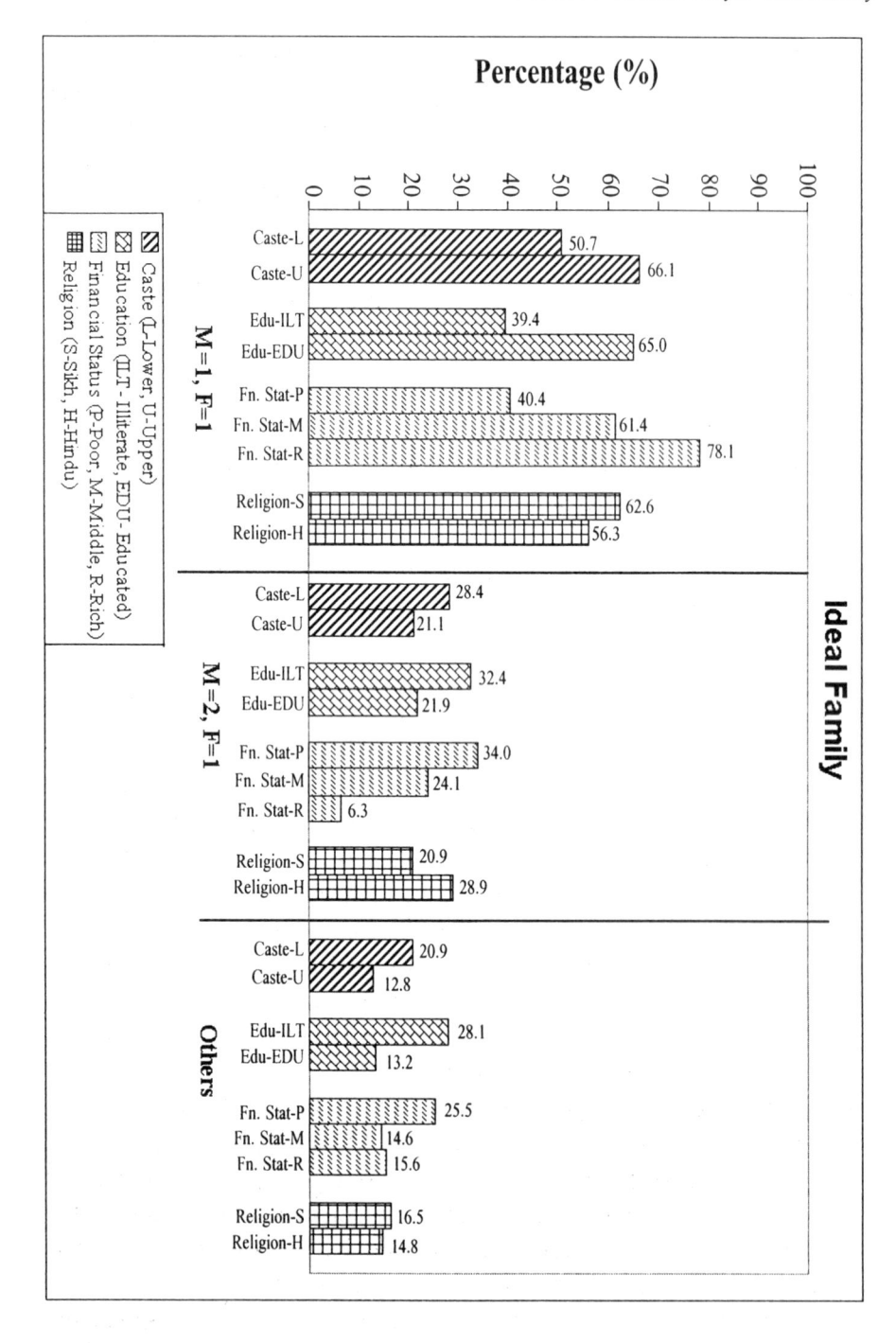

Ideal Family

M=1, F=1

Category	Value
Caste-L	50.7
Caste-U	66.1
Edu-ILT	39.4
Edu-EDU	65.0
Fn. Stat-P	40.4
Fn. Stat-M	61.4
Fn. Stat-R	78.1
Religion-S	62.6
Religion-H	56.3

M=2, F=1

Category	Value
Caste-L	28.4
Caste-U	21.1
Edu-ILT	32.4
Edu-EDU	21.9
Fn. Stat-P	34.0
Fn. Stat-M	24.1
Fn. Stat-R	6.3
Religion-S	20.9
Religion-H	28.9

Others

Category	Value
Caste-L	20.9
Caste-U	12.8
Edu-ILT	28.1
Edu-EDU	13.2
Fn. Stat-P	25.5
Fn. Stat-M	14.6
Fn. Stat-R	15.6
Religion-S	16.5
Religion-H	14.8

Legend: Caste (L-Lower, U-Upper); Education (ILT-Illiterate, EDU-Educated); Financial Status (P-Poor, M-Middle, R-Rich); Religion (S-Sikh, H-Hindu)

Analysis

Table IV : Number of Female Children at the time of Abortion

Categories	No. of Respondents	Two or More	Less then Two	Chi-Square Test
Caste:				
Lower	148	100 (67.6%)	48 (32.4%)	$\chi^2 = 7.05$
Upper	218	117 (53.7%)	101 (46.3%)	Significant
Education:				
Illiterate	71	52 (73.2%)	19 (26.8%)	$\chi^2 = 6.85$
Educated	302	170 (56.3%)	132 (43.7%)	Significant
Financial Status:				
Poor	47	37 (78.7%)	10 (21.3%)	$\chi^2 = 13.63$
Middle	295	178 (60.3%)	117 (39.7%)	Significant
Rich	32	12 (37.5%)	20 (62.5%)	
Religion:				
Sikh	230	124 (53.9%)	106 (46.1%)	$\chi^2 = 6.81$
Hindu	142	96 (67.6%)	46 (32.4%)	Significant

Observations

- I have tried to see what was the size of family, that is number of children sex-wise when the respondent went for abortion. This not only indicates how strong is the desire to have a son, but also how blatant one is in following this method of female foeticide. Women who went for female foeticide when they already had two or more daughters can be said to be less crude and blatant in their approach than those who went for female foeticide, when they were having only one or no daughter.
- The findings completely negate the common perception that people belonging to lower strata of the society are more crude in their behaviour and have lesser human values, therefore, they are more into this act of female foeticide. The truth is otherwise. Women belonging to upper strata of the society are more brutal in their approach, because more number of them have undergone female foeticide when they had less than two daughters. 79% of poor went for female foeticide when they had two or more

daughters, against this, the percentage of rich is less than half of it, similarly 73% of illiterate waited for at least two daughters against only 56% of educated before undergoing female foeticde. Greater percentage of lower castes went for female foeticide when they had two or more daughters.

- One possible defence for people from upper social stratum can be that since they are financially better, they can easily afford the abortion which costs Rs. 5,000-10,000/- whereas, people from lower social stratum do not have this money and they prefer to wait before going for female foeticide. Another possible argument in favour of rich, educated, upper caste can be that they are more particular about smaller family, therefore, they go for female foeticide at an early stage.

Analysis 53

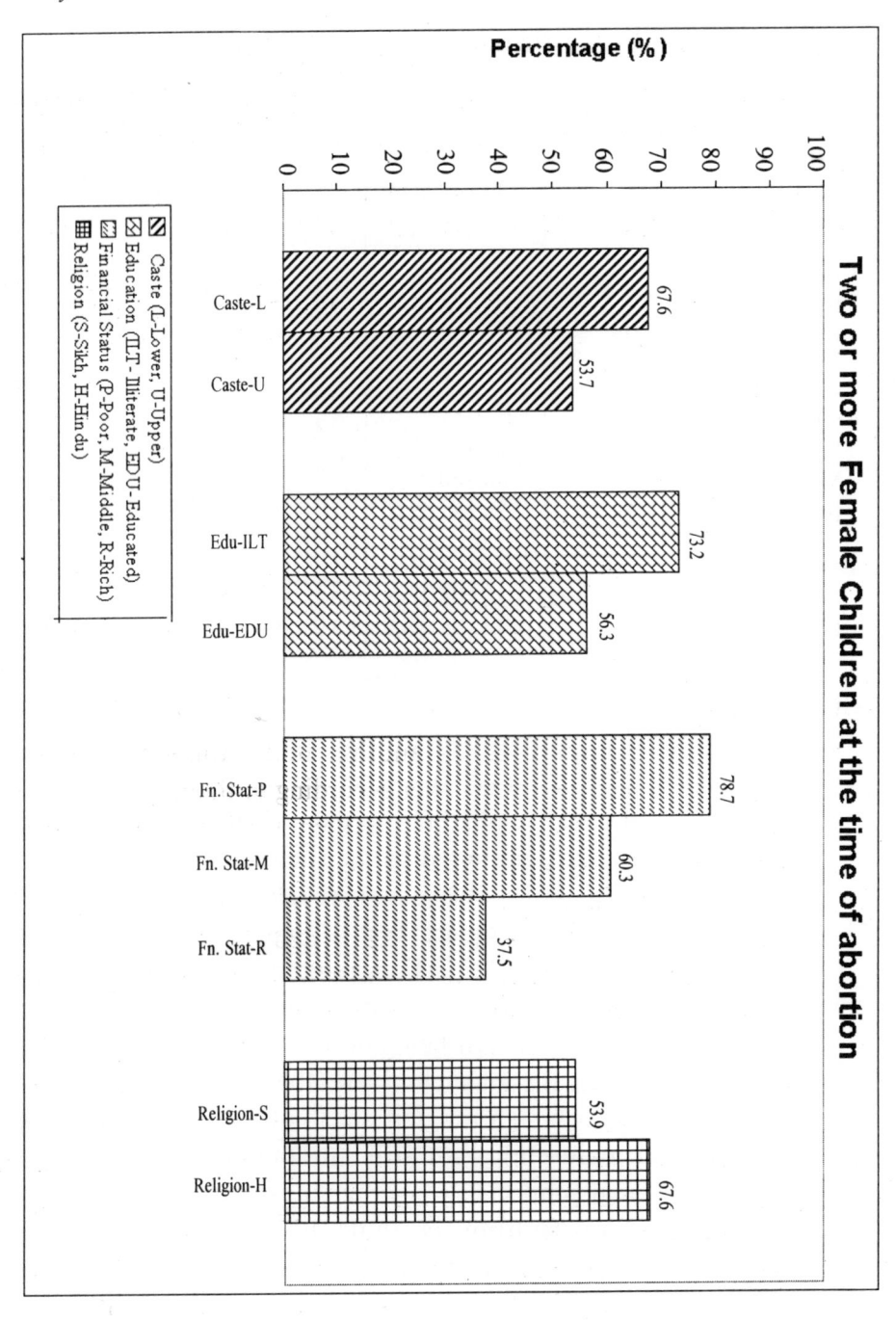

Two or more Female Children at the time of abortion

Category	Percentage (%)
Caste-L	67.6
Caste-U	53.7
Edu-ILT	73.2
Edu-EDU	56.3
Fn. Stat-P	78.7
Fn. Stat-M	60.3
Fn. Stat-R	37.5
Religion-S	53.9
Religion-H	67.6

Legend:
- Caste (L-Lower, U-Upper)
- Education (ILT- Illiterate, EDU- Educated)
- Financial Status (P-Poor, M-Middle, R-Rich)
- Religion (S-Sikh, H-Hindu)

Table V : Preference to Male Child

Categories	No. of Respondents	Yes	No	Chi-Square Test
Caste:				
Lower	148	133 (89.9%)	15 (10.1%)	$\chi^2 = 0.016$
Upper	218	195 (89.4%)	23 (10.6%)	Insignificant
Education:				
Illiterate	71	60 (84.5%)	11 (15.5%)	$\chi^2 = 2.38$
Educated	302	274 (90.7%)	28 (9.3%)	Insignificant
Financial Status:				
Poor	47	41 (87.2%)	6 (12.8%)	$\chi^2 = 0.53$
Middle	295	266 (90.2%)	26 (8.8%)	Insignificant
Rich	32	28 (87.5%)	4 (12.5%)	
Religion:				
Sikh	230	212 (92.2%)	18 (7.8%)	$\chi^2 = 3.75$
Hindu	142	122 (85.9%)	20 (14.1%)	Insignificant

Observations

- Preference to male child is another name for gender bias. Respondents were asked whether according to them society gave preference to the male child. 90% of them replied in affirmative, saying that boys were preferred by the society.
- One expected that gender bias is less prevalent amongst educated and rich, but when Chi-Square Test is applied to this data, this myth is exploded. Caste, education, religion and financial status of the family do not affect data on gender bias. This means education and financial well being do not change the attitude of the society towards the male child, and they equally suffer from 'sons' syndrome. Though religion does not have any impact on preference to male child, but still, in comparison to Hindus, preference to male child is stronger amongst the Sikhs.
- One interesting finding is that though education has "insignificant" affect on gender bias, still amongst educated class preference to male child is stronger in comparison to the illiterate class. 90.7% of educated respondents reported gender bias against 84.5% of the illiterate respondents.

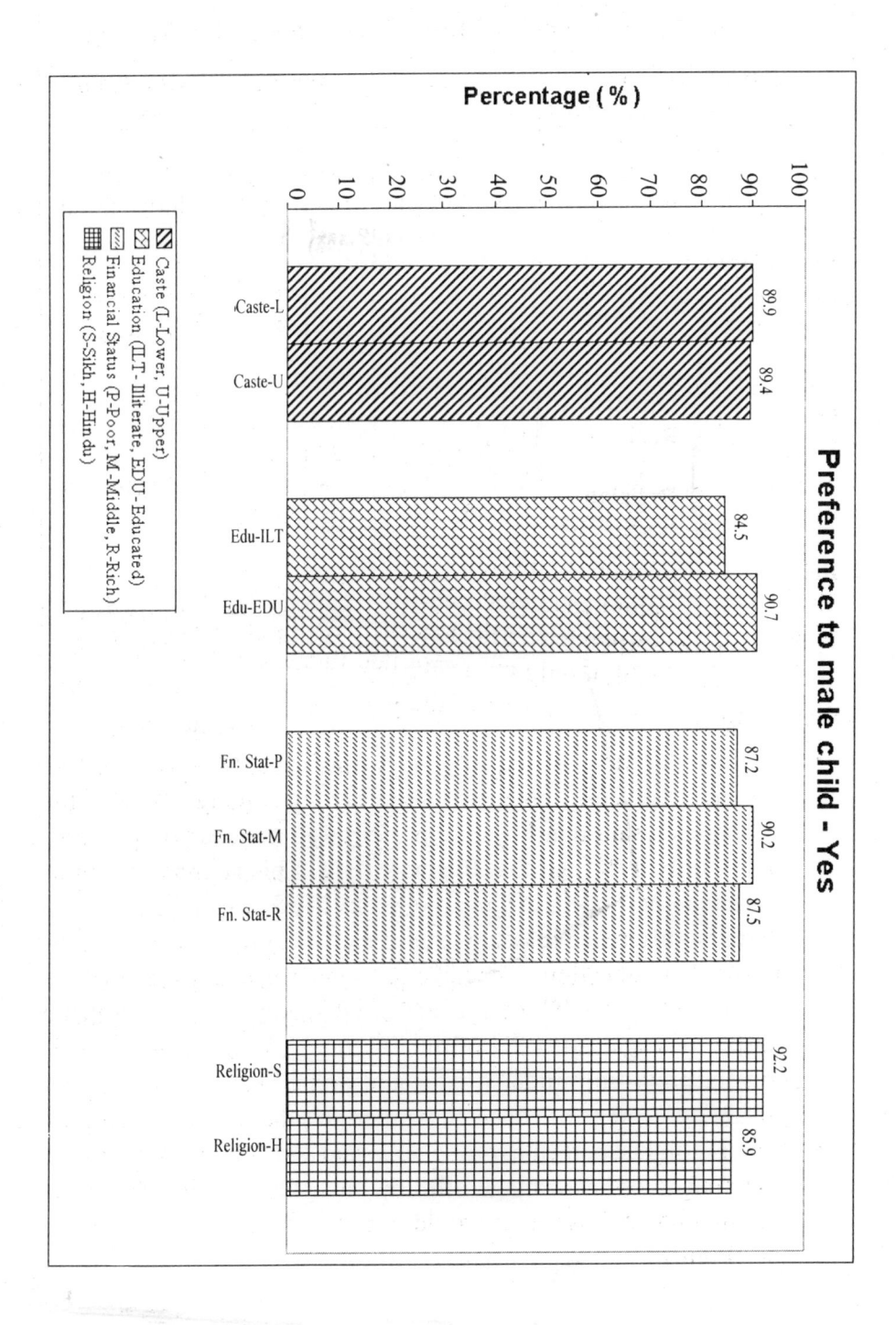

Analysis

Preference to male child - Yes

Category	Percentage (%)
Caste-L	89.9
Caste-U	89.4
Edu-ILT	84.5
Edu-EDU	90.7
Fn. Stat-P	87.2
Fn. Stat-M	90.2
Fn. Stat-R	87.5
Religion-S	92.2
Religion-H	85.9

Legend:
- Caste (L-Lower, U-Upper)
- Education (ILT- Illiterate, EDU- Educated)
- Financial Status (P-Poor, M-Middle, R-Rich)
- Religion (S-Sikh, H-Hindu)

Table VI: Preference to Male Child - Right Or Wrong

Categories	No. of Respondents	Right	Wrong	Chi-Square Test
Caste:				
Lower	148	63 (42.6%)	85 (57.4%)	$\chi^2 = 1.49$
Upper	218	79 (36.2%)	139 (63.8%)	Insignificant
Education:				
Illiterate	71	39 (54.9%)	32 (45.1%)	$\chi^2 = 9.18$
Educated	302	107 (35.4%)	195 (64.6%)	Significant
Financial Status:				
Poor	47	19 (40.4%)	28 (59.6%)	$\chi^2 = 0.90$
Middle	295	117 (39.7%)	178 (60.3%)	Insignificant
Rich	32	10 (31.3%)	22 (68.7%)	
Religion:				
Sikh	230	82 (35.7%)	148 (64.3%)	$\chi^2 = 2.8$
Hindu	142	63 (44.4%)	79 (55.6%)	Insignificant

Observations

- Another question related to gender bias asked was whether the preference given to boys is right or wrong. Though 90% of the respondents said that boys are preferred in the society (previous table), only 40% said that this was right. This is encouraging as more than half of the women do believe in sex equality.
- Here the difference in data is significant only for education. This means that education does have an impact on the psyche of the women. Only 35.4% of the educated women have supported gender bias against 54.9% of the illiterate. Though gender bias is equally prevalent amongst educated and illiterate families, but greater percentage of educated women felt that it was not correct.
- Though higher percentage of Sikhs said that the boys are given preference, less percentage of them have supported gender bias, thus amongst Sikhs things would improve faster in comparison to the Hindus.

Analysis 57

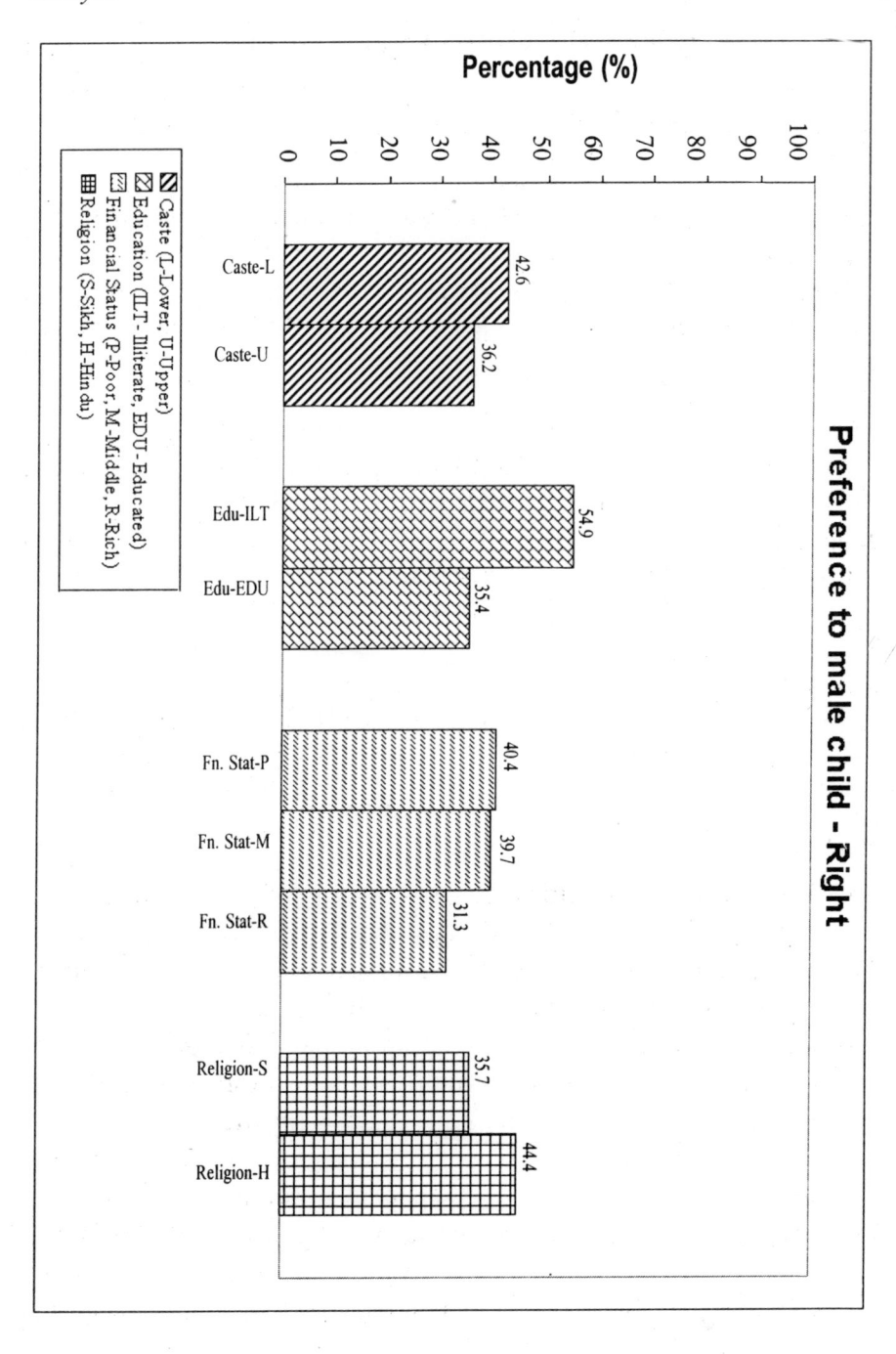

Preference to male child

Category	Percentage (%)
Caste-L	42.6
Caste-U	36.2
Edu-ILT	54.9
Edu-EDU	35.4
Fn. Stat-P	40.4
Fn. Stat-M	39.7
Fn. Stat-R	31.3
Religion-S	35.7
Religion-H	44.4

Legend:
- Caste (L-Lower, U-Upper)
- Education (ILT- Illiterate, EDU-Educated)
- Financial Status (P-Poor, M-Middle, R-Rich)
- Religion (S-Sikh, H-Hindu)

Table VII : Consent For Abortion

Categories	No. of Respondents	Yes	No	Chi-Square Test
Caste:				
Lower	148	49 (33.0%)	99 (66.9%)	$\chi^2 = 8.01$
Upper	218	43 (19.7%)	175 (80.3%)	Significant
Education:				
Illiterate	71	20 (28.2%)	51 (71.8%)	$\chi^2 = 0.58$
Educated	302	72 (23.8%)	230 (76.2%)	Insignificant
Financial Status:				
Poor	47	9 (19.1%)	38 (80.9%)	$\chi^2 = 1.09$
Middle	295	76 (25.8%)	219 (74.2%)	Insignificant
Rich	32	7 (21.9%)	25 (78.1%)	
Religion:				
Sikh	230	55 (24.0%)	175 (76.0%)	$\chi^2 = 0.22$
Hindu	142	37 (26.0%)	105 (74.0%)	Insignificant
Level of Decision:				
Low	155	24 (15.5%)	131 (84.5%)	$\chi^2 = 18.48$
Middle	92	22 (24.0%)	70 (76.0%)	Significant
High	121	46 (38.0%)	75 (62.0%)	

Observations

- This was the most critical question asked to the respondents. It is very important to know whether the mother willingly went for female foeticide or she was pressurised and forced into this act. Here also common perception is totally negated by the findings of the study. The common perception is that, since there is hardly any complaint from any woman for being forced into female foeticide, these abortions take place with the consent of the woman. One must appreciate that social problems such as female foeticide have multiple dimensions to it and normally there are very few complaints. For example, we all know that dowry is very common in our society and a large number of young girls and parents succumb to dowry demands, but there is hardly any complaint.
- Most important finding of the study is, that in only 25% cases, female foeticide was done with the consent of the mother. In 75%

of the cases, respondent was pressurised by her husband, in-laws and parents. The pressure was mostly from husband, followed by in-laws and other relatives.

- Another common belief is, that since people of lower social stratum are more crude in their behaviour, and have higher propensity to force their women into such acts. This myth is exploded by this study. When Chi-Square Test is applied to categories, such as education, financial status of the family, and religion, the impact of these categories is insignificant on the data of number of women who had consented for abortion. This means that statistically as far as pressurising their women for female foeticide is concerned, the behaviour of illiterate and educated, that of poor and rich, and that of Sikh and Hindu, is the same. In fact, greater percentage of illiterate respondents had consented for foeticide, in comparison to their educated counterparts. This reflects on the double standards in the upper class.

- Another important finding is that the data is significantly affected by caste, that is, caste of the respondent has an impact on whether the woman had willingly undergone female foeticide or not. Amongst lower caste 33% women willingly went for abortion in comparison to 19.7% of upper caste. This completely negates the common perception that people belonging to lower strata of the society are "less cultured". Here, the truth is otherwise.

- The biggest impact on this data is the respondents' level of decision making in the family. The respondents were asked what decisions they could take in the family and accordingly they have been categorised into low, middle, high level of decision making. In cases of women having higher level of decision making in the family, consent cases are 38%, against this only 15.5% of women having low level of decision making had consented for abortion. This clearly shows that empowerment of women is the real solution to this menace. Since in 75% of the total cases, women are forced for abortion, if women are empowered and they have higher level of decision making in the society, the percentage of women, who are forced into female foeticide would drastically decrease. One disturbing finding is that more number of women of upper social stratum, who are supposed to be the path bearers are pressurised and forced into female foeticide.

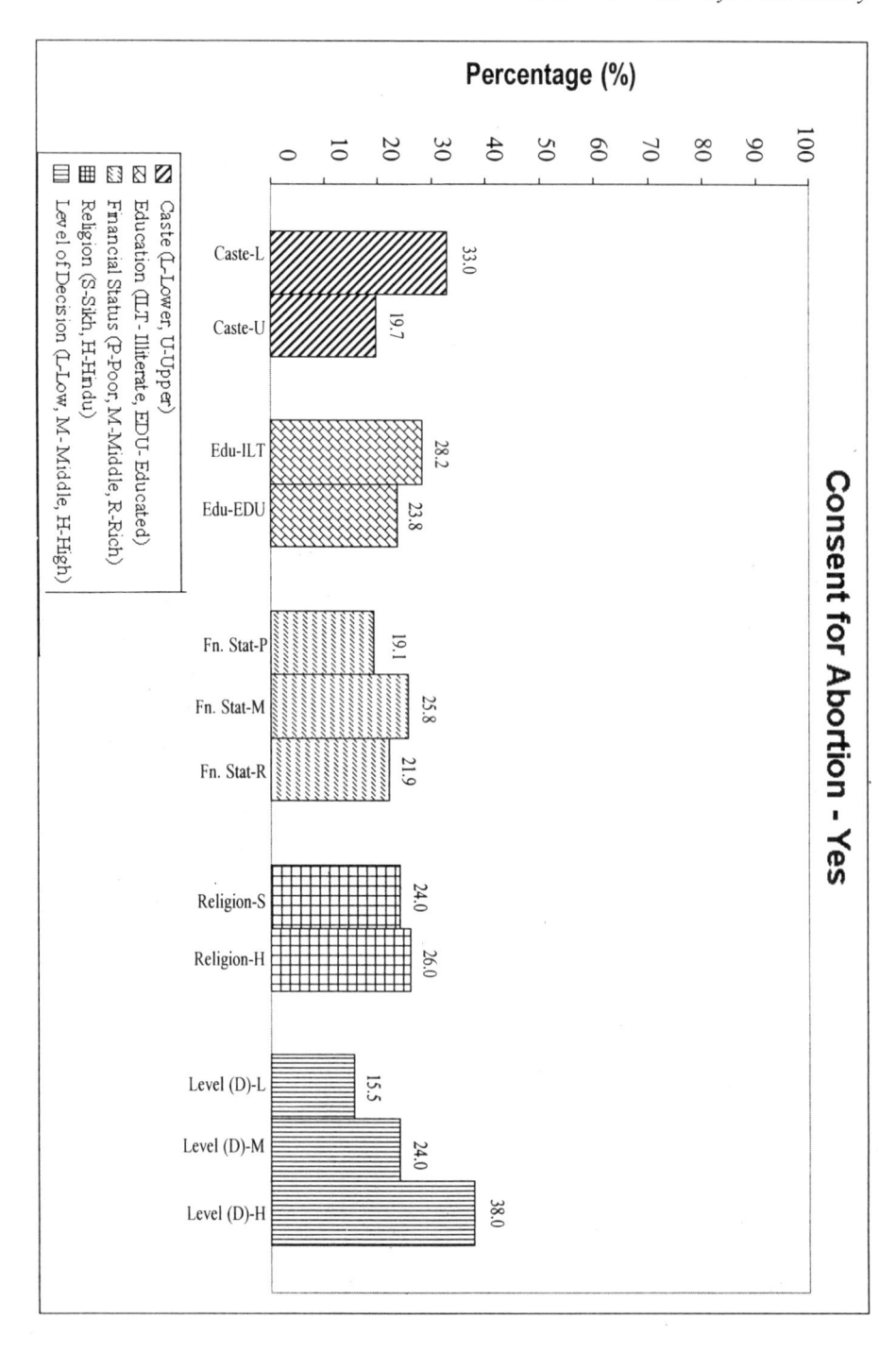

Female Foeticide: Myth and Reality

Consent for Abortion - Yes

Category	Percentage (%)
Caste-L	33.0
Caste-U	19.7
Edu-ILT	28.2
Edu-EDU	23.8
Fn. Stat-P	19.1
Fn. Stat-M	25.8
Fn. Stat-R	21.9
Religion-S	24.0
Religion-H	26.0
Level (D)-L	15.5
Level (D)-M	24.0
Level (D)-H	38.0

Legend:
- Caste (L-Lower, U-Upper)
- Education (ILT- Illiterate, EDU- Educated)
- Financial Status (P-Poor, M-Middle, R-Rich)
- Religion (S-Sikh, H-Hindu)
- Level of Decision (L-Low, M-Middle, H-High)

Analysis

Table VIII : Sin to Kill Female Foetus

Categories	No. of Respondents	Yes	No	Chi-Square Test
Caste:				
Lower	148	126 (85.1%)	22 (14.9%)	$\chi^2 = 0.29$
Upper	218	181 (83.0%)	37 (17.0%)	Insignificant
Education:				
Illiterate	71	56 (78.9%)	15 (21.1%)	$\chi^2 = 0.97$
Educated	302	253 (83.8%)	49 (16.2%)	Insignificant
Religion:				
Sikh	230	186 (80.9%)	44 (19.1%)	$\chi^2 = 4.83$
Hindu	142	127 (89.4%)	15 (10.6%)	Significant
Religious Status:				
Not Religious	35	27 (77.1%)	8 (22.9%)	$\chi^2 = 1.99$
Religious	114	186 (83.0%)	38 (17.0%)	Insignificant
Very Religious	224	99 (86.8%)	15 (13.2%)	

Observations:

- When 2001 census data on sex ratio was published, it sent shock waves all over. Sex ratio in Punjab was consistently rising from 1911 till 1991, but in 2001 it showed a decline, not only this, age specific sex ratio for 0-6 years age group was even worse. Immediately there was very strong religious advocacy by every one. The presumption was, that women who undergo female foeticide, do not know that it is a sin and if they were made to realise this, they would not do it. This myth has been exploded by the study, as 84% of the respondents said that they knew it is a sin to kill female foetus.
- Let us see what happens when Chi-Square Test is applied to this data. The impact of caste, education, and religious status is insignificant on number of women saying that female foeticide is a sin. This is rather surprising, because one would expect that education would have a positive impact on this response and at least those who visit place of worship more frequently, should

have this realisation in greater number. But it is not so. This shows that religious dimension to female foeticide is deeply rooted in our psyche, and it is fundamental to our thinking and perception.

- This is a big set back for our policy makers who made religious advocacy core of their strategy to combat the menace of female foeticide. The present form of religious advocacy is not going to work. It needs to be modified, for example, monopoly of males in religious ceremonies should go, our thinking that only sons carry family name, and that daughters are 'paraya dhan' (someone else's wealth) must change.

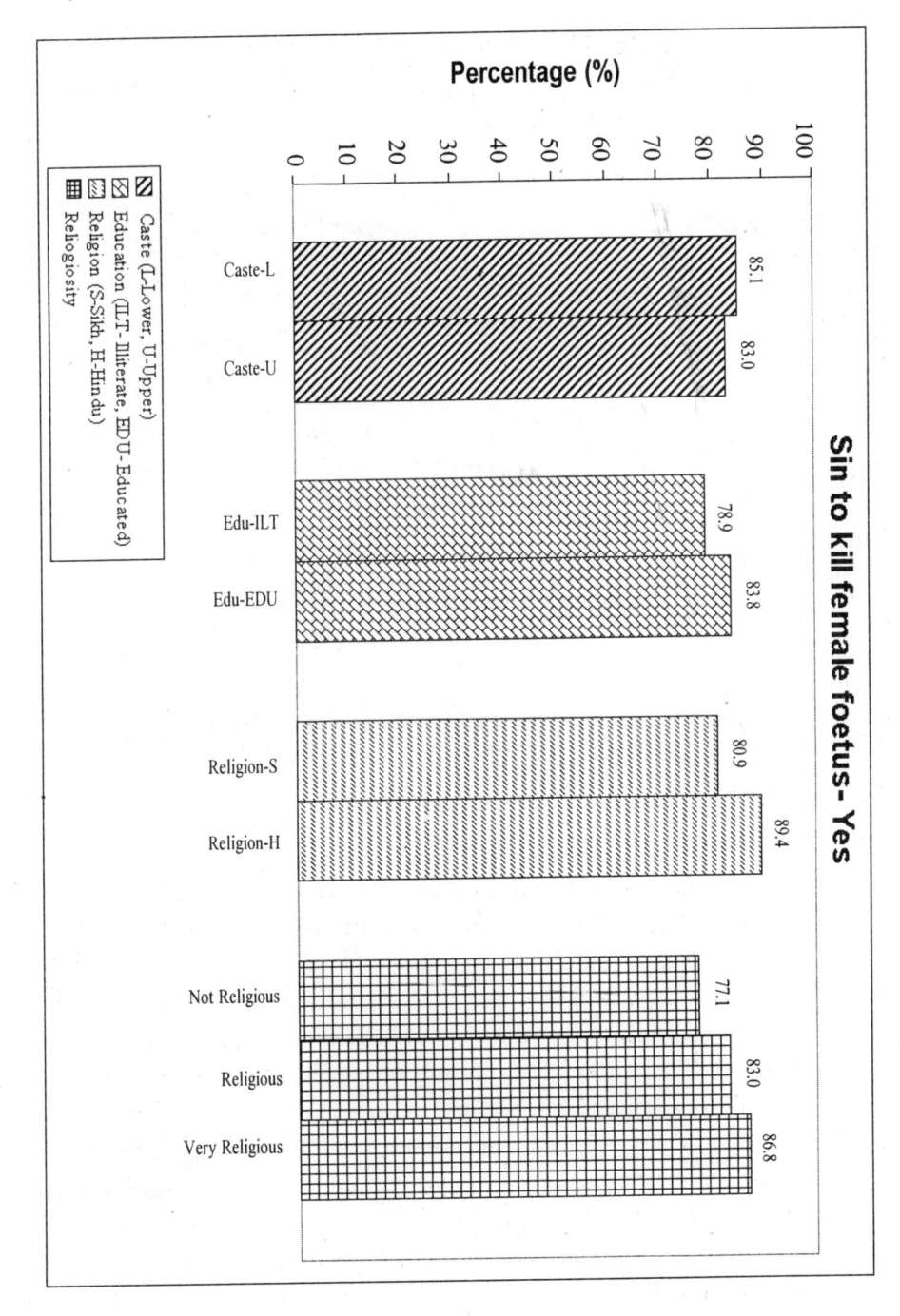

Analysis

Sin to kill female foetus - Yes

Category	Percentage (%)
Caste-L	85.1
Caste-U	83.0
Edu-ILT	78.9
Edu-EDU	83.8
Religion-S	80.9
Religion-H	89.4
Not Religious	77.1
Religious	83.0
Very Religious	86.8

Legend:
- Caste (L-Lower, U-Upper)
- Education (ILT- Illiterate, EDU- Educated)
- Religion (S-Sikh, H-Hindu)
- Religiosity

Table IX : Regret After Abortion

Categories	No. of Respondents	Yes	No	Chi-Square Test
Caste:				
Lower	148	89 (60.1%)	59 (39.9%)	$\chi^2 = 0.78$
Upper	218	141 (64.7%)	77 (35.3%)	Insignificant
Education:				
Illiterate	71	41 (57.7%)	30 (42.3%)	$\chi^2 = 0.93$
Educated	302	193 (63.9%)	109 (36.1%)	Insignificant
Financial Status:				
Poor	47	27 (57.4%)	20 (42.6%)	$\chi^2 = 3.48$
Middle	295	192 (65.1%)	103 (34.9%)	Insignificant
Rich	32	16 (50.0%)	16 (50.0%)	
Religion:				
Sikh	230	149 (64.8%)	81 (35.2%)	$\chi^2 = 0.91$
Hindu	142	85 (59.9%)	57 (40.1%)	Insignificant
Religious Status:				
Not Religious	35	20 (57.1%)	15 (42.9%)	$\chi^2 = 0.97$
Religious	224	139 (62.1%)	85 (37.9%)	Insignificant
Very Religious	114	75 (65.8%)	39 (34.2%)	

Observations:

- Respondents were asked whether they regret having undergone female foeticide, 63% of them have answered in affirmative.
- One significant feature of this data is that, it is not significantly affected by any category, that is, caste, education, financial status, religion and religious status do not have any impact on the feeling of regret. This shows that feeling of regret, which is interplay of various socio-economic factors, is deeply rooted in the psyche of the women and even education and financial status of the family do not have any impact. Though women of upper social stratum, that is, those who are educated, financially better off, upper caste have higher percentage (64%) reporting regrets after abortion in comparison to their counterparts (58%), but statistically the difference is not significant and it can be attributed to chance factor alone.

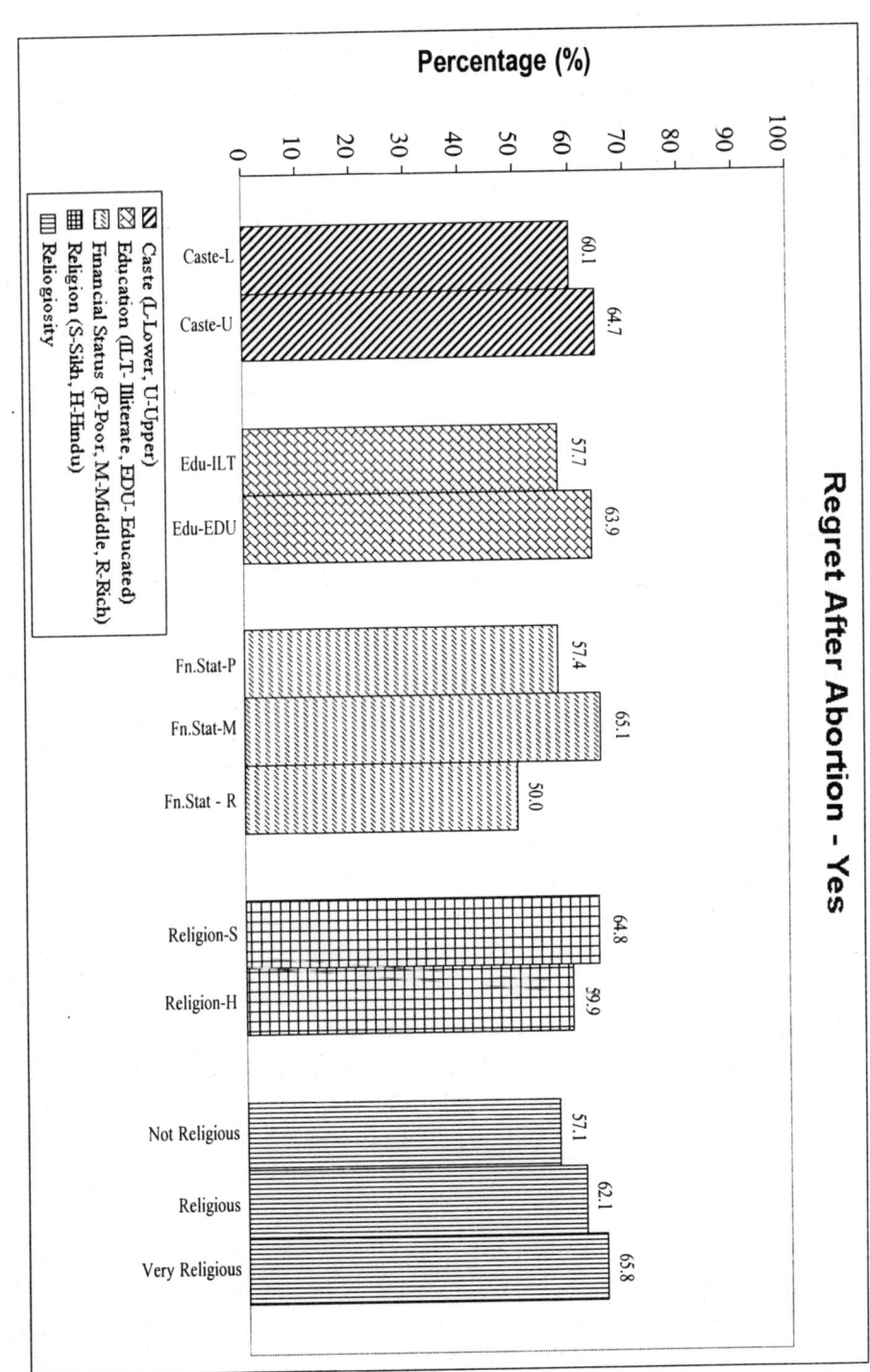

Analysis

Regret After Abortion - Yes

Category	Percentage (%)
Caste-L	60.1
Caste-U	64.7
Edu-ILT	57.7
Edu-EDU	63.9
Fn.Stat-P	57.4
Fn.Stat-M	65.1
Fn.Stat-R	50.0
Religion-S	64.8
Religion-H	59.9
Not Religious	57.1
Religious	62.1
Very Religious	65.8

Legend:
- Caste (L-Lower, U-Upper)
- Education (ILT- Illiterate, EDU- Educated)
- Financial Status (P-Poor, M-Middle, R-Rich)
- Religion (S-Sikh, H-Hindu)
- Religiosity

Table X : Repeat Abortion

Categories	No. of Respondents	Yes	No	Chi-Square Test
Caste:				
Lower	148	47 (31.8%)	101 (68.2%)	$\chi^2 = 0.24$
Upper	218	64 (29.4%)	154 (70.6%)	Insignificant
Education:				
Illiterate	71	28 (39.4%)	43 (60.6%)	$\chi^2 = 3.92$
Educated	302	83 (27.5%)	219 (72.5%)	Significant
Financial Status				
Poor	47	9 (19.1%)	38 (80.9%)	$\chi^2 = 3.50$
Middle	295	94 (31.9%)	201 (68.1%)	Insignificant
Rich	32	8 (25.0%)	24 (75.0%)	
Religion:				
Sikh	230	62 (26.9%)	168 (73.1%)	$\chi^2 = 2.39$
Hindu	142	49 (34.5%)	93 (65.5%)	Insignificant
Religious Status:				
Not Religious	35	10 (28.6%)	25 (71.4%)	$\chi^2 = 0.09$
Religious	224	68 (30.4%)	156 (69.6%)	Insignificant
Very Religious	114	33 (28.9%)	81 (71.1%)	

Observations:

- 30% of the respondents said that they would repeat female foeticide to have a male child. This percentage is less than those who do not regret having undergone the abortion (37%). This shows that some of the women who, though do not regret the abortion, but still they do not want to repeat the act.
- This data is significantly affected by education. 39.4% of illiterate women intend to repeat female foeticide in comparison to 27.5% of their educated counterpart. This shows education does have an impact on the psyche of the women, though not as such, as one would hope for.
- Caste, financial status, religion, religious status do not have any impact on this aspect of female foeticide. What is surprising is that even women who are very religious and those who are not religious have similar approach towards female foeticide. This further reinforces the earlier finding of the study that religion is not an important factor in female foeticide.

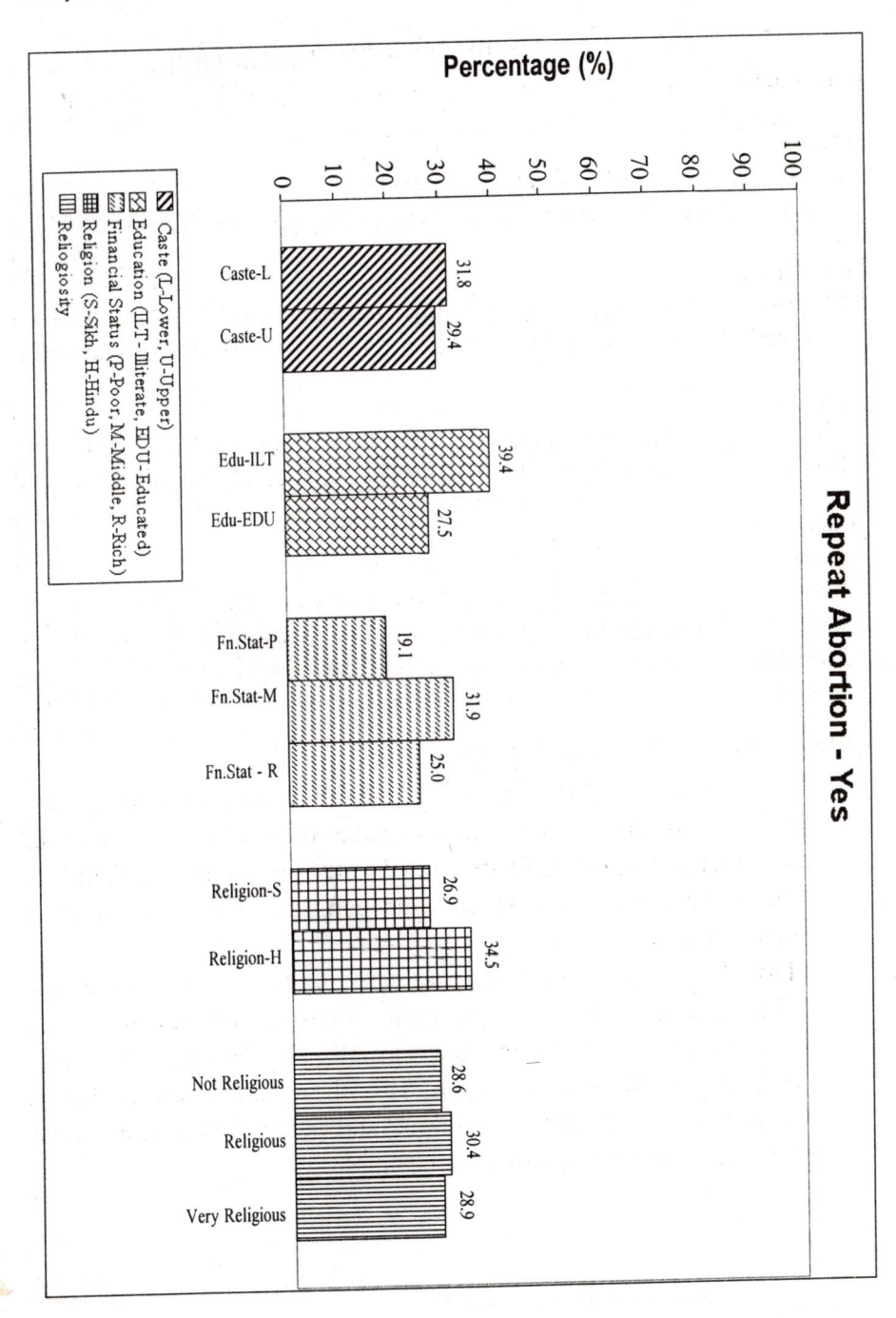

Analysis

Repeat Abortion - Yes

Legend:
- Caste (L-Lower, U-Upper)
- Education (ILT- Illiterate, EDU- Educated)
- Financial Status (P-Poor, M-Middle, R-Rich)
- Religion (S-Sikh, H-Hindu)
- Reliogiosity

Category	Percentage (%)
Caste-L	31.8
Caste-U	29.4
Edu-ILT	39.4
Edu-EDU	27.5
Fn.Stat-P	19.1
Fn.Stat-M	31.9
Fn.Stat-R	25.0
Religion-S	26.9
Religion-H	34.5
Not Religious	28.6
Religious	30.4
Very Religious	28.9

Table XI : No. of Tries for Male Child

Categories	1	2	3	>=4	Chi-Square Test
Caste:					
Lower	20 (17.3%)	34 (29.3%)	41 (35.3%)	21 (18.1%)	$\chi^2 = 1.37$
Upper	24 (15.7%)	49 (32.0%)	46 (30.1%)	34 (22.2%)	Insignificant
Education:					
Illiterate	7 (13.0%)	17 (31.5%)	16 (29.6%)	14 (25.9%)	$\chi^2 = 1.47$
Educated	37 (16.7%)	68 (30.6%)	74 (33.3%)	43 (19.4%)	Insignificant
Religion:					
Sikh	28 (16.9%)	58 (34.9%)	50 (30.1%)	30 (18.1%)	$\chi^2 = 4.05$
Hindu	16 (14.8%)	27 (25.0%)	40 (37.0%)	25 (23.2%)	Insignificant
Financial Status:					
Poor	10 (29.4%)	7 (20.6%)	10 (29.4%)	7 (20.6%)	$\chi^2 = 7.96$
Middle	33 (15.1%)	69 (31.7%)	72 (33%)	44 (20.2%)	Insignificant
Rich	1 (4.2%)	9 (37.5%)	8 (33.3%)	6 (25.0%)	

Observations:

- Women were asked how many times they would try for a male child. More than 60% of them said that they would try 2-3 times and a large number of them wanted to try for even more than four times. This shows the level of desperation in the society for a male child.

- This data is not significantly affected by any of the categories. This means, lower and upper caste, illiterate and educated, Sikh and Hindu, rich and poor, they are all alike when it comes to multiple abortions to get a son. This shows that socio-economic factors, which govern the thinking and perception of the women for a son are deeply rooted.

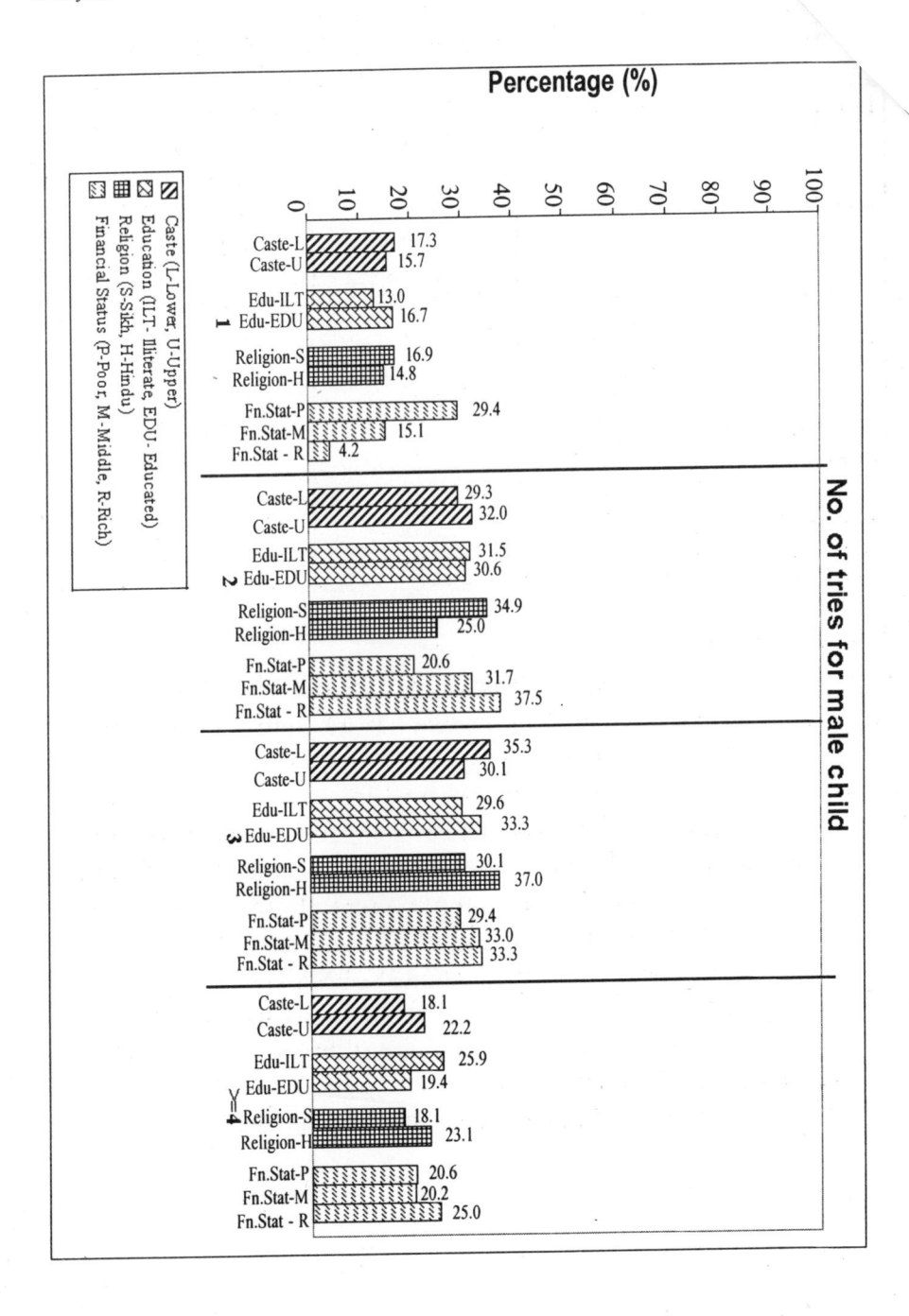

Analysis

Legend:
- Caste (L-Lower, U-Upper)
- Education (ILT- Illiterate, EDU- Educated)
- Religion (S-Sikh, H-Hindu)
- Financial Status (P-Poor, M-Middle, R-Rich)

No. of tries for male child

1
Category	Percentage (%)
Caste-L	17.3
Caste-U	15.7
Edu-ILT	13.0
Edu-EDU	16.7
Religion-S	16.9
Religion-H	14.8
Fn.Stat-P	29.4
Fn.Stat-M	15.1
Fn.Stat-R	4.2

2
Category	Percentage (%)
Caste-L	29.3
Caste-U	32.0
Edu-ILT	31.5
Edu-EDU	30.6
Religion-S	34.9
Religion-H	25.0
Fn.Stat-P	20.6
Fn.Stat-M	31.7
Fn.Stat-R	37.5

3
Category	Percentage (%)
Caste-L	35.3
Caste-U	30.1
Edu-ILT	29.6
Edu-EDU	33.3
Religion-S	30.1
Religion-H	37.0
Fn.Stat-P	29.4
Fn.Stat-M	33.0
Fn.Stat-R	33.3

4
Category	Percentage (%)
Caste-L	18.1
Caste-U	22.2
Edu-ILT	25.9
Edu-EDU	19.4
Religion-S	18.1
Religion-H	23.1
Fn.Stat-P	20.6
Fn.Stat-M	20.2
Fn.Stat-R	25.0

What is More Relevant-Caste or Religion

	Category	Chi-Square (for α=.05)	Remark
Education	Caste	16.11	Highly significant
	Religion	1.54	Insignificant
Financial status	Caste	34.73	Highly significant
	Religion	4.17	Insignificant
Level of decision making	Caste	7.00	Significant
	Religion	1.91	Insignificant
Employment	Caste	1.33	Insignificant
	Religion	0.02	Insignificant

Observations

- Religion and caste are the two big realities of our society. It is ironical that though an individual has no control over these two things, still religion and caste stick to him the moment he is born and he carries them throughout his life.
- I have tried to analyse whether caste and religion have any impact on various development indices such as education, financial status of the family, and employment status of the woman. Religion has insignificant impact on these development indices, this shows that level of development of Sikhs and Hindus is the same. But this data is highly significant for caste. More number of women belonging to lower caste are illiterate and poor. Despite positive discrimination by the government in favour of lower caste, there is still big gap between the upper caste and the lower caste.

Analysis

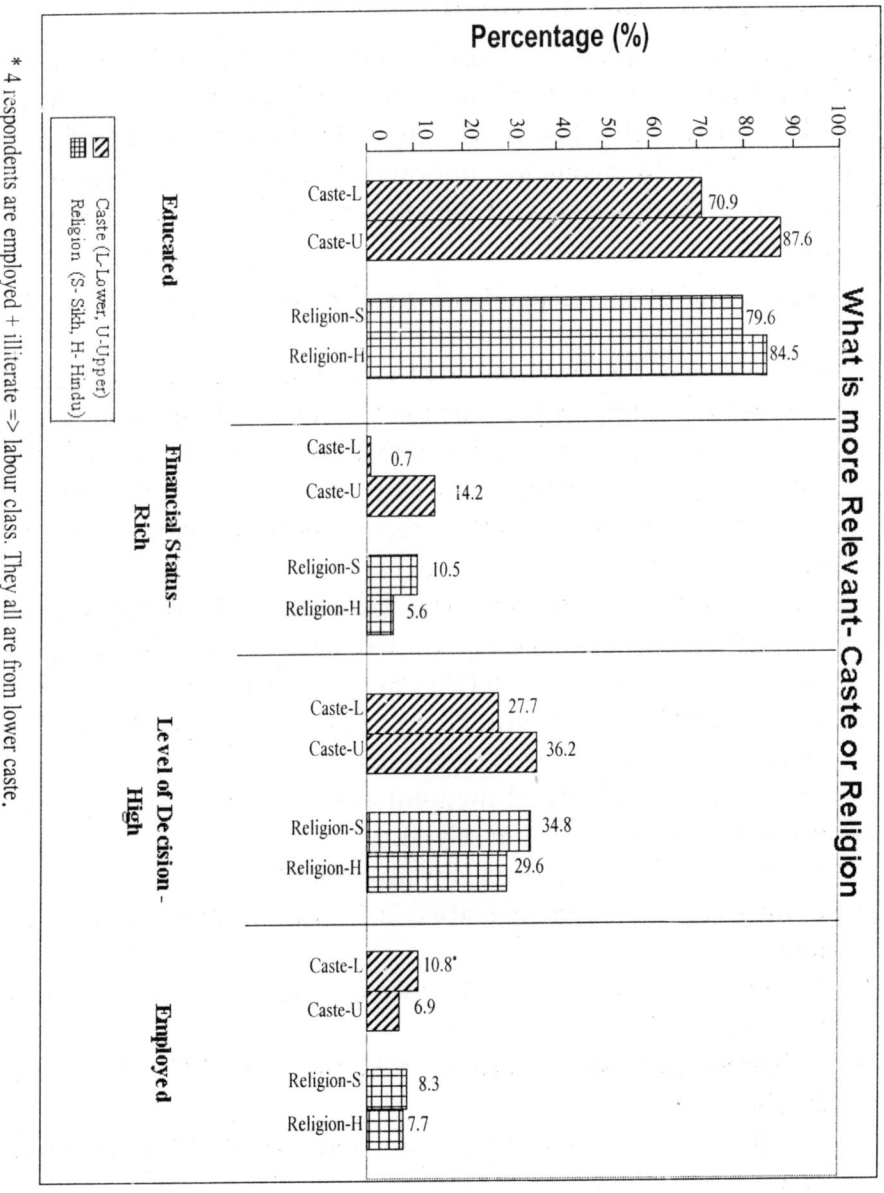

What is more Relevant- Caste or Religion

Educated
- Caste-L: 70.9
- Caste-U: 87.6
- Religion-S: 79.6
- Religion-H: 84.5

Financial Status- Rich
- Caste-L: 0.7
- Caste-U: 14.2
- Religion-S: 10.5
- Religion-H: 5.6

Level of Decision - High
- Caste-L: 27.7
- Caste-U: 36.2
- Religion-S: 34.8
- Religion-H: 29.6

Employed
- Caste-L: 10.8*
- Caste-U: 6.9
- Religion-S: 8.3
- Religion-H: 7.7

Legend:
- Caste (L-Lower, U-Upper)
- Religion (S- Sikh, H- Hindu)

* 4 respondents are employed + illiterate => labour class. They all are from lower caste.

4.4 Summary and Conclusion

1. Sample and it's Characteristics

The sample comprised of 374 case histories. A total of 500 women, who had undergone female foeticide were interviewed by the volunteers of the ISS – Istri Sehat Sabhas (Women Health Groups). 126 forms were rejected due to incomplete information. Respondents were from all the 17 districts of the state of Punjab. They were mostly from rural and semi urban areas.

- **Age:** Most of the respondents were in the age group of 20-30 years
  63% were married between 18-21 years Still a large number, 12% got married below 18 years that is the minimum permissible age for marriage. Common belief is that upper caste, educated and rich marry at higher age, but surprisingly the data on age at marriage is not significantly affected by these socio-economic parameters.
- **Education, level of decision making and employment:** 71(19%) respondents were illiterate, 276 (74%) were undergraduate, and only 26 (7%) were graduates. Their husbands were slightly better educated - 52 (14%) illiterate, 285 (76%) undergraduate, and 36(10%) graduates.
  42% had low, 25% had medium and 33% had high level of decision making in the household.
  341 (92%) of the respondents were unemployed.
- **Family and it's financial status:** 207 (56%) respondents lived in joint families.
  47 (12%) were poor, 295 (79%) were middle class, and 32 (9%) were rich.
- **Religion and Caste:** 230 (61%) were Sikh, and 142 (38%) were Hindu.
  218 (60%) were from upper caste, and 148 (40%) from lower caste.
- **Religious status:** 35 (9%) were not religious, 224 (60%) were religious, and 114 (31%) were very religious. Hindu and Sikh were equally religious. Upper caste, educated and rich were more religious.

Analysis

- **Awareness about prenatal testing:** There is universal awareness about sex determination. 84% had prior knowledge about it. Major source of information was advertisements, followed by family members and health workers.

  62% of the respondents were of the opinion that mother should know the sex of the unborn child, majority of them (89%) were of the view that this would help them in choosing the desired sex of their child and thus help in limiting the family size. 38% were against sex determination, majority of them (40%) felt that this information may increase mental tension during the pregnancy, 31% felt that there would be pressure to abort female foetus.

- **No. of children and pregnancies:** 76% had upto 3 living children, 14% had 4 or more children. As against this, 45% had upto 3 pregnancies, and 28% had 5 or more pregnancies. At the time of interview, 62% had no male child. 73% had 1 or 2 living female child, however, 8 (2%) did not have a female child. Subsequent births after the birth of the male child were very low.

- **Ideal family size:** All the respondents desired at least 1 male child. 67% wanted to have 1 male child, 31% wished 2 male children. 97% desired to have at least 1 female child, 87% wanted only 1 female child.

  Most of them wanted to have small family. 60% desired 1 son and 1 daughter, 26% wanted 2 sons and 1 daughter. This data was significantly effected by caste, education and financial status. Upper caste, educated and rich wanted to have smaller families.

- **Sex of the first child:** 56% felt that first child should be male, whereas, 40% said it could be any. Majority who preferred male child gave reason that it relieved mother from the worries about the sex of the subsequent child. Vast majority (86%) did not opt for sex determination during first pregnancy.

- **Feeling before and after sonography:** 87% respondents were either worried or apprehensive before sex determination. 33% were sad and 62% were tense after they were informed about the female foetus.

- **Maltreatment for not having a male child:** 77% did not report any maltreatment for not having a male child. Of those who reported maltreatment, 90% felt mentally tortured and 10% were physically abused.

Female Foeticide: Myth and Reality

ed abortions: 1 induced abortion was reported by 81% as against this 15% had 2 induced abortions. 1 case reported re than 4 induced abortions. Duration of pregnancy was 3-6 months at the time of abortion.

When they opted for induced abortion, 39% had 1 female child, 38% had 2 female children, 21% had 3 or more female children. In 7 cases (2%) there was no female child at the time of abortion.

2. Caste vs Religion

Even today, caste is one of the most relevant factors in our society. Development indices such as education, employment, financial status, level of decision making of women in the household, are greatly effected by the caste factor. More number of lower caste are illiterate, unemployed, and poor. Conversely, religion does not significantly effect these development indices.

3. Gender bias

Gender bias, that is ultimately responsible for female foeticide, is deeply rooted in our psyche. 90% of the respondents agreed that boys are given preference in the society, however, only 40% felt that this social attitude was justified. Various reasons have been cited for giving preference to boys. 36% thought that boys were preferred because they carry family name, 21% felt that boys are needed for looking after in the old age, 16% were of the view that boys enhanced respect in the society. Very few gave financial reasons, only 3% said that girls are a financial liability.

84% had the perception that postnatal care of the mother was much better after the male child. More than 90% felt that having a male child enhanced woman's status in the society.

Religion, education, financial well-being and religiosity do not effect the attitude towards the male child. However, more number of educated respondents said that preference to male child was not correct.

4. Consent for female foeticide

Since there are hardly any complaints, most of us think that foeticide is always with the consent of the mother and that amongst less educated and poor who care little for human values, women are forced for abortion. The study completely negates this 'common sense'.

Analysis

Consent cases are only 25%. Educated and rich are in no way better than their counter parts. Upper castes are worse in this case as more number of upper caste women are forced for abortion. Consent cases in upper caste are 19% against 33% in case of lower caste. One parameter that quite significantly effects this data is level of decision making of the mother in the household. 38% of those who could take major decisions in the family consented for foeticide, against this only 15% of those who had low level of decision making reported consent for foeticide. This shows that empowerment of the women should be the key strategy to combat the menace of female foeticide.

5. Reasons for female foeticide

71% of the respondents went for female foeticide because they previously had daughters and now they wanted a son. Only 6% said that daughters were a financial liability. This belies the common perception that female foeticide is primarily due to financial reasons, such as dowry. Respondents were not against daughters, but they wanted atleast one or two sons in the family. This finding is also supported by the fact that very few went for sex determination at the time of first pregnancy and that hardly any one desired only sons. Most of the respondents desired 1 son and 1 daughter or 2 sons and 1 daughter. Thus, preference for male child with desire for small family, is the biggest reason for this menace.

6. Religious advocacy

When census data on sex ratio came, everybody thought that those who go for sex determination and female foeticide perhaps do not realise that foeticide is a sin and that if they are told that it is a sin, they would not do it. So there was very strong religious advocacy by all religious leaders. But one major finding of the study is that 84% already realised that foeticide was a sin. This data is not effected by caste and education. Surprisingly, the data is not significantly effected by the religiosity of the respondent, that is, very religious and irreligious had similar response. Thus, present form of religious advocacy is not going to work. Religious advocacy need to be modified, for example, women should be allowed to participate equally in all religious rituals, it should be emphasised that daughters also carry family name.

7. Feeling of regret

60% of the respondents regret having undergone foeticide. This data is not significantly effected by caste, education, religion, religiosity, and financial status. 30% of the respondents said that they would repeat this act. This data is significantly effected by education with less number of educated wanting to repeat it (27.5%), therefore, education does have an impact, though not much.

8. Number of tries for male child

Though only 30% said they would repeat female foeticide, large number of them said they would further try for a male child (277). More than 60% of them wanted to try for 2-3 times. Quite a large number of them (15%) wanted to try for 4 or more number of times. This data is not significantly effected by caste, religion, education, and financial status.

"Female foeticide is a complex issue. Women who have undergone this procedure, have quite different perception from what medical professionals, religious leaders, opinion makers, gatekeepers of the society, and planners think. Since education, financial well being, religiosity do not have much impact on the psyche of the women who have undergone female foeticide, to combat this menace, state must empower women by affirmative discrimination in their favour."

Annexure - I

ਪ੍ਰਸ਼ਨਾਵਲੀ

1.) ਜ਼ਿਲਾ ....ਹੁਸ਼ਿਆਰ ਪੁਰ................

2.) ਇਸਤਰੀ ਦੀ ਕ੍ਰਮ ਨੰਬਰ ....354..........

3.) ਵਿਆਹ ਹੋਏ ਨੂੰ ਸਾਲ ...14.....................

4.) ਵਿਦਿਆ :   ੳ) ਅਨਪੜ੍ਹ
                     ਅ) ਪੰਜ ਪਾਸ ✓
                     ੲ) ਦਸ ਪਾਸ
                     ਸ) ਬੀ.ਏ ਜਾਂ ਉਪਰ

5.) ਕਿੱਤਾ : ਘਰ ਦਾ ਕੰਮ ✓ / ਨੌਕਰੀ ਪੇਸ਼ਾ
ਜੇਕਰ ਨੌਕਰੀ ਹੈ ਤਾਂ ਆਮਦਨ:

6.) ਪਤੀ ਦੀ ਵਿਦਿਅਕ ਪੱਧਰ :
                     ੳ) ਅਨਪੜ੍ਹ
                     ਅ) ਪੰਜ ਪਾਸ ✓
                     ੲ) ਦਸ ਪਾਸ
                     ਸ) ਬੀ.ਏ ਜਾਂ ਉਪਰ

7.) ਪਰਵਾਰ ਦੀ ਆਰਥਕ ਪੱਧਰ:

ਖੇਤੀ ਲਈ ਜ਼ਮੀਨ	:	2/5/10/15 ਕਿੱਲੇ ਜਾਂ ਵੱਧ ਪ ਕੈਲੇ ✗
ਆਪਣਾ ਘਰ	:	ਕੱਚਾ/ਪੱਕਾ ✗
ਘਰ ਦੇ ਕਮਰੇ	:	1/2/3 ਜਾਂ ਵੱਧ ✗
ਬਿਜਲੀ	:	ਹਾਂ/ਨਹੀਂ ✗
ਗੈਸ	:	ਹਾਂ/ਨਹੀਂ ✗
ਟੈਲੀਵੀਜ਼ਨ	:	ਹਾਂ/ਨਹੀਂ ✓
ਸਵਾਰੀ	:	ਨਹੀਂ/ਸਾਈਕਲ/ਸਕੂਟਰ/ਕਾਰ/ਟਰੈਕਟਰ
ਰੇਡੀਓ	:	ਹਾਂ/ਨਹੀਂ ✗
ਸਾਂਝਾ ਪਰਵਾਰ	:	ਹਾਂ/ਨਹੀਂ

8.) ਜਾਤ :

9.) ਧਰਮ :

10.) ਕੀ ਤੁਸੀਂ ਗੁਰਦੁਆਰੇ/ਮੰਦਰ ਜਾਂਦੇ ਹੋ ?   ਹਰ ਰੋਜ਼/ਹਫਤੇ ਬਾਦ/ਮਹੀਨੇ ਬਾਦ/ ਕਦੀ ਨਹੀਂ ✓

11.) ਜੀਵਤ ਬੱਚਿਆਂ ਦੀ ਗਿਣਤੀ ਅਤੇ ਉਮਰ:

ਮੁੰਡੇ	ਇੱਕ × ਦੋ × ਤਿੰਨ ×	ਉਮਰ × 1. × 2. × 3. ×
ਕੁੜੀਆਂ	ਇੱਕ ਦੋ ✓ ਤਿੰਨ	1. 6 ਸਾਲ × 2. 12 ਸਾਲ × 3.

12.) ਤੁਸੀਂ ਕਿੰਨੇ ਵਾਰ ਗਰਭਧਾਰਨ ਕੀਤਾ ਹੈ   4 ਵਾਰ

13.) ਕੀ ਕਿਸੇ ਬੱਚੇ ਦੀ ਮੌਤ ਵੀ ਹੋਈ ਹੈ   ਹਾਂ/ਨਹੀਂ ✓

14.) ਜੇਕਰ ਹਾਂ ਤਾਂ :   ਮੌਤ ਸਮੇਂ ਬੱਚੇ ਦੀ ਉਮਰ____ ×
                    ਬੱਚਾ ਕੁੜੀ ਸੀ ਜਾਂ ਮੁੰਡਾ____ ×
                    ਮੌਤ ਦਾ ਕਾਰਨ_____

15.) ੳ) ਤੁਹਾਡੇ ਵਿਚਾਰ ਵਿਚ ਕਿੰਨੇ ਬੱਚੇ ਹੋਣੇ ਚਾਹੀਦੇ ਹਨ: 1/2/3/4 ਜਾਂ ਵੱਧ ✓
     ਅ) ਇਹਨਾਂ ਵਿਚੋਂ ਕਿੰਨੀਆ ਕੁੜੀਆਂ ਅਤੇ ਕਿੰਨੇ ਮੁੰਡੇ ਹੋਣੇ ਚਾਹੀਦੇ ਹਨ :
        ਮੁੰਡੇ   1
        ਕੁੜੀਆਂ 1

16.) ਤੁਹਾਡੇ ਵਿਚਾਰ ਵਿਚ ਬੱਚੇ ਦਾ ਮੁੰਡਾ ਜਾਂ ਕੁੜੀ ਹੋਣਾ ਕਿਸ ਤੇ ਨਿਰਭਰ ਕਰਦਾ ਹੈ:
        ਰੱਬ ✓
        ਪਤੀ
        ਪਤਨੀ

17.) ਕੀ ਤੁਸੀ ਜਾਣਦੇ ਹੈ ਕਿ ਜਨਮ ਤੋਂ ਪਹਿਲਾਂ ਪੇਟ ਵਿਚ ਪਲ ਰਿਹਾ ਬੱਚਾ ਮੁੰਡਾ ਹੈ ਜਾਂ ਕੁੜੀ ਦਾ ਪਤਾ ਲਗ ਸਕਦਾ ਹੈ ?   ਹਾਂ/ਨਹੀਂ
     ਜੇਕਰ ਹਾਂ ਤਾਂ ਕਿਵੇਂ

```
ਅਲਟਰਾ ਸਾਊਂਡ ਮਸ਼ੀਨ ਦੇ ਚੈੱਕਅੱਪ ਨਾਲ ਵੀ ਤੇ ਕੁਝ ਕੁ ਪੜਾਅ ਵੱਖਰੇ
ਹੋਣ ਦੀ ਵੀ ਹਨ ਜਿਸ ਤੋਂ ਪਤਾ ਲਗਦਾ ਹੈ ਕਿ ਬੱਚਾ ਮੁੰਡਾ ਹੈ ਜਾਂ ਕੁੜੀ
```

Annexure-I

18.) ਤੁਹਾਨੂੰ ਇਹ ਜਾਣਕਾਰੀ ਕਿੱਥੋਂ ਮਿਲੀ: ਸਿਹਤ ਕਰਮਚਾਰੀ
ਪਤੀ
ਰਿਸਤੇਦਾਰ ✓
ਰਵਾਦੀ
ਅਖਬਾਰਾਂ/ ਇਸ਼ਤਿਹਾਰ ✓
ਕੰਧ ਚਿੱਤਰ ✓

19.) ਤੁਹਾਡੇ ਵਿਚਾਰ ਵਿਚ ਜਨਮ ਤੋਂ ਪਹਿਲਾਂ ਬੱਚੇ ਦਾ ਕੁੜੀ ਜਾਂ ਮੁੰਡਾ ਹੋਣ ਦਾ ਪਤਾ ਲਗਾ ਜਾਣਾ ਚੰਗਾ ਹੈ? ਹਾਂ/ਨਹੀਂ ✓
ਆਪਣੇ ਪੱਖ ਦੀ ਪੁਸ਼ਟੀ ਲਈ ਕਾਰਨ ਦੱਸੋ

> [handwritten response]

20.) ਕੀ ਤੁਹਾਡੇ ਵਿਚਾਰ ਵਿਚ ਸਮਾਜ ਵਿਚ ਮੁੰਡਿਆਂ ਨੂੰ ਕੁੜੀਆਂ ਨਾਲੋਂ ਜਿਆਦਾ ਤਰਜੀਹ ਦਿੱਤੀ ਜਾਂਦੀ ਹੈ?
ਹਾਂ ✓/ਨਹੀਂ
ਜੇਕਰ ਹਾਂ ਤਾਂ ਕੀ ਤੁਹਾਡੇ ਵਿਚਾਰ ਵਿਚ ਇਹ ਰਵੱਈਆ ਸਹੀ ਹੈ?   ਹਾਂ/ਨਹੀਂ ✓
ਜੇਕਰ ਹਾਂ ਤਾਂ ਕਾਰਨ ਦੱਸੋ?

21.) ਕੀ ਤੁਹਾਡੇ ਵਿਚਾਰ ਵਿਚ ਪੁੱਤਰ ਦੇ ਜਨਮ ਨਾਲ ਇਸਤਰੀ ਦਾ ਘਰ ਵਿਚ ਸਨਮਾਨ ਵੱਧ ਜਾਂਦਾ ਹੈ? ਹਾਂ ✓/ਨਹੀਂ
ਜੇਕਰ ਹਾਂ ਤਾਂ ਕਿਵੇਂ

> [handwritten response]

22.) ਕੀ ਪ੍ਰਸੂਤਰ ਨੂੰ ਜਨਮ ਦੇਣ ਵਾਲੀ ਇਸਤਰੀ ਦਾ ਨਿਯਮਤ ਧਿਆਨ ਰਖਿਆ ਜਾਂਦਾ ਹੈ ? ਹਾਂ/ਨਹੀਂ
ਅਗਰ ਹਾਂ ਤਾਂ ਕਿਵੇਂ

> ਰਤੀ ਅਸਾਂ ਪਿੰਡਾ ਸ਼ੁਰਾ ਕੋਲ ਮਸੀ ਇਸਤਰੀ ਦਾ ਧਿਆਨ ਰਿਖਾ
> ਇਹ ਕਰੇ ਰਹਿਆ ਸਾਲਾ ਤੋਂ ਪਿਛੇ ਜਾਂਦੇ ਦਾ ਨਾਨੀ ਅਸੀ
> ਪਤੀ ਦੀਆਂ ਇਕ ਸੀਰ। ਜਾਂ ਦਾ ਧਿਆਨ ਠਹੀ ਰਖਾ ਦੀ
> ਪੀਰ ਹਿਊਂ।

23.) ਤੁਸੀਂ ਪਰਵਾਰ ਵਿਚ ਕਿਹੜੇ ਫੈਸਲੇ ਆਪਣੇ ਆਪ ਲੈ ਸਕਦੇ ਹੋ?
- ਅਜ ਕਿਹੜੀ ਦਾਲ/ਸਬਜ਼ੀ ਬਣਾਉਣੀ ਹੈ। ✓
- ਆਪਣਾ ਇਲਾਜ ਕਿਸ ਸਰੂ ਤੋਂ ਕਰਵਾਉਣਾ ਹੈ। ✗
- ਗਰਭ ਕਦੋਂ ਧਾਰਨ ਕਰਨਾ ਹੈ। ✗
- ਕਪਿੜਾ ਅਤੇ ਹੋਰ ਘਰ ਦੀਆ ਵਰਤੀਆਂ ਰੀਜਾ ਖਰੀਦਣ ਸੰਬਧੀ ਫੈਸਲਾ ਲੈਣਾ। ✗
- ਖੇਤੇ ਜਾਣ ਲਈ ✗

24.) ਤੁਹਾਡੇ ਵਿਚਾਰ ਵਿਚ ਪਰਿਵਾਰ ਵਿਚ ਕੀ ਹੋਣਾ ਚਾਹੀਦਾ ਹੈ ? ਲੜਕਾ/ਲੜਕੀ /ਕੋਈ ਵੀ ✓
ਆਪਣੇ ਪੱਖ ਦੀ ਪੁਸ਼ਟੀ ਲਈ ਕਾਰਨ ਦਸੋ

> ਜਰਦ ਸਾਡੇ ਪਰਿਵਾਰ ਸਮਾ ਤੇ ਰਹਿਣਾ ਤਾਂ ਦਰਨੀ ਪੁੱਤ ਸ਼ੁਰੂ ਹੀ
> ਤੇ ਸੀਦੇ ਹੋਇ ਹੈ। ਕਿਉਂਕਿ ਦਰਨਾ ਤਾਂ ਪਹਿਲਾ ਤੇ ਹਿਆ ਹੈ/
> ਲਡੀ ਕਰ ਤਾਂ ਦਰਨੀ ਤੇ ਹਾਹੀ ਹੈ।

25.) ਕੀ ਤੁਸੀ ਪਹਿਲੇ ਕਦਮ ਸਮੇਂ ਬੱਚੇ ਦੇ ਯੁਰੀ ਜਾਂ ਮੁੰਡੇ ਹੋਣ ਦਾ ਪਤਾ ਲਗਾਉਣ ਲਈ ਅਲਟਰਾ ਸਾਊਂਡ ਕਰਵਾਇਆ ਸੀ ? ਹਾਂ/ਨਹੀਂ ✓

26.) ਕੀ ਪ੍ਰਸੂਤਰ ਨੂੰ ਜਨਮ ਨਾ ਦੇਣ ਕਾਰਨ ਤੁਹਾਡੇ ਨਾਲ ਬੁਰਾ ਸਲੂਕ ਕੀਤਾ ਕਿਆ ਹੈ? ਹਾਂ/ਨਹੀਂ ✓
ਅਗਰ ਹਾਂ ਤਾਂ ਕਿਸ ਤਰ੍ਹਾਂ ਦਾ :

> ਜਾਂ ਕਿਉਂਕਿ ਸੀਰੇ ਸ਼ੁਰੇ ਅਸਰੇ ਨਾਲ ਹਿਣ ਜਦਰੇ ਰਹਿਣ ਸੀ।
> ਰਤੀ ਕ ਭੁਰਾ ਜਲਾਕਿਆ।

Annexure-I 81

27.) ਕੀ ਤੁਸੀਂ ਪੁੱਤਰ ਦੀ ਚਾਹ ਪੂਰੀ ਕਰਨ ਲਈ ਕਿਸੇ ਸੰਤ-ਮਹਾਤਮਾ ਕੋਲ ਗਏ ਜਾਂ ਕੋਈ ਦਵਾਈ-ਬੂਟੀ ਦੀ ਵਰਤੋ ਕੀਤੀ ਹੈ?   ਹਾਂ/ਨਹੀਂ
ਜੇਕਰ ਹਾਂ ਤਾਂ ਤੁਹਾਨੂੰ ਕੀ ਕਰਨ ਲਈ ਕਿਹਾ ਗਿਆ?

> ਬਾਬਾ ਪਿਤਾ ਜੀ ਤੂੰਹੀ ਜਿੰਨੂ ਕਰਮੀ ਮਾ ਵਰੇ ਦਿਨ ਤਕ ਭੇਟ ਤੁਰੇਗੀ।

28.) ਕੀ ਤੁਹਾਡਾ ਕੋਈ ਗਰਭ ਗਿਰਿਆ ਹੈ?   ਹਾਂ/ਨਹੀਂ
ਜੇਕਰ ਹਾਂ ਤਾਂ
- ਕਿੰਨੇ ਗਰਭ ਆਪਣੇ ਆਪ ਗਿਰੇ __1__
- ਕਿੰਨੇ ਗਰਭ ਗਿਰਵਾਏ ਗਏ __2__
- ਜੇਕਰ ਗਰਭ ਗਿਰਾਏ ਗਏ ਤਾਂ ਕੀ ਕਾਰਨ ਸੀ :
   - ਡਾਕਟਰੀ ਕਾਰਨ
   - ਕੁੜੀ ਦਾ ਪਤਾ ਲਗਣ ਕਾਰਨ ✓
- ਸਫਾਈ ਕਰਵਾਉਣ ਸਮੇਂ ਕਿੰਨੇ ਮਹੀਨੇ ਦਾ ਗਰਭ ਸੀ? __4 ਮਹੀਨੇ__
- ਉਸ ਸਮੇਂ ਜੀਵਤ ਲੜਕੇ ਅਤੇ ਲੜਕੀਆਂ ਦੀ ਗਿਣਤੀ __2__
   - ਲੜਕੇ __X__
   - ਲੜਕੀਆਂ __2__

29.) ਕੀ ਸਫਾਈ ਕਰਵਾਉਣ ਤੋਂ ਪਹਿਲਾਂ ਅਲਟਰਾ ਸਾਊਂਡ(ਬੱਚੇ ਦਾ ਲਿੰਗ ਜਾਣਨ ਲਈ)ਕਰਵਾਇਆ ਸੀ : ਹਾਂ/ਨਹੀਂ
ਜੇਕਰ ਹਾਂ ਤਾਂ ਇਹ ਕਿਸ ਦੇ ਕਹਿਣ ਤੇ ਕਰਵਾਇਆ?
- ਤੁਹਾਡੀ ਆਪਣੀ ਮਰਜ਼ੀ ਸੀ
- ਤੁਹਾਡੇ ਪਤੀ ਨੇ ਕਿਹਾ ਸੀ ✓
- ਤੁਹਾਡੇ ਸੱਸ-ਸਹੁਰੇ ਨੇ ਕਿਹਾ ਸੀ
- ਤੁਹਾਡੇ ਮਾਤਾ-ਪਿਤਾ ਨੇ ਕਿਹਾ ਸੀ
- ਤੁਹਾਡੀ ਕਿਸੇ ਸਹੇਲੀ ਨੇ ਕਿਹਾ ਸੀ
- ਕਿਸੇ ਸਿਹਤ ਕਰਮਚਾਰੀ ਨੇ ਕਿਹਾ ਸੀ
- ਜਾਂ ਕਿਸੇ ਹੋਰ ਨੇ

ਜੇਕਰ ਆਪਣੀ ਮਰਜ਼ੀ ਸੀ ਤਾਂ ਕਾਰਨ ਦੱਸੋ:

30.) ਲੜਕਾ ਜਾਂ ਲੜਕੀ ਦੇ ਪਤਾ ਕਰਨ ਲਈ ਅਲਟਰਾਸਾਊਂਡ ਕਰਵਾਉਣ ਤੋਂ ਪਹਿਲਾਂ ਤੁਸੀਂ ਕੀ ਮਹਿਸੂਸ ਕਰਦੇ ਸੀ ?

ਕੁਝ ਖਾਸ ਨਹੀਂ / ਕੋਈ ਚਿੰਤਾ ਸੀ / ਕੋਈ ਡਰ–ਭੈਅ ਸੀ ✓

31.) ਜਦੋਂ ਤੁਹਾਨੂੰ ਇਹ ਪਤਾ ਲੱਗਾ ਕਿ ਪੇਟ ਵਿੱਚ ਲੜਕੀ ਹੈ ਤਾਂ ਤੁਹਾਡੀ ਕੀ ਮਨਿਸਥਾ ਕਰਨਾ ਸੀ ?

ਕੁਝ ਖਾਸ ਨਹੀਂ / ਨਿਰਾਸ਼ਾ ਹੋਈ / ਦਿਮਾਗ ਤੇ ਬੋਝ ਦੇ ਰਿਹਾ / ਡਰ ਮਹਿਸੂਸ ਹੋਣ ਲੱਗਿਆ ।

32.) ਕੀ ਤੁਸੀ ਗਰਭਪਾਤ ਇਹ ਜਾਨਣ ਤੋਂ ਬਾਅਦ ਕਰਵਾਇਆ ਕਿ ਬੱਚਾ ਲੜਕੀ ਹੈ ? ਹਾਂ/ਨਹੀਂ
ਜੇਕਰ ਹਾਂ ਤਾਂ ਕਿਉਂ ?

_____
_____
_____

33.) ਟੈਸਟ ਕਰਵਾਉਣ ਤੋਂ ਬਾਅਦ ਤੁਸੀਂ ਕਿਸ ਦੇ ਕਹਿਣ ਤੇ ਗਰਭਪਾਤ ਕਰਵਾਇਆ?

* ਆਪਣੀ ਮਰਜ਼ੀ ਨਾਲ
* ਪਤੀ ✓
* ਮਾਤਾ-ਪਿਤਾ
* ਸੱਸ-ਸਹੁਰਾ
* ਰਿਸ਼ਤੇ ਦਾਰ
* ਕਿਸੇ ਹੋਰ ਦੇ ਕਹਿਣ ਤੇ

34.) ਕੀ ਤੁਸੀ ਗਰਭਪਾਤ ਕਰਵਾਉਣਾ ਚਾਹੁੰਦੇ ਸੀ ? ਹਾਂ/ਨਹੀਂ
ਜੇਕਰ ਹਾਂ ਤਾਂ ਕਿਉਂ ?

_____
_____
_____

35.) ਕੀ ਤੁਹਾਡੇ ਕਿਸੇ ਰਿਸ਼ਤੇਦਾਰ ਨੇ ਲਿੰਗ ਨਿਰਧਾਰਨ ਕਰਵਾਉਣ ਬਾਅਦ ਪੇਟ ਵਿਚ ਕੁੜੀ ਹੋਣ ਕਾਰਨ ਗਰਭਪਾਤ ਕਰਵਾਇਆ ਹੈ ?/ ਹਾਂ/ਨਹੀਂ

Annexure-I

36.) ਕੀ ਤੁਹਾਨੂੰ ਗਰਭਪਾਤ ਕਰਵਾਉਣ ਤੋਂ ਬਾਅਦ ਕੋਈ ਅਫਸੋਸ ਹੋਇਆ ਹੈ ?   ਹਾਂ/ਨਹੀਂ ✓

37.) ਤੁਹਾਡੇ ਵਿਚਾਰ ਅਨੁਸਾਰ ਕੀ ਲੜਕੀ ਨੂੰ ਗਰਭ ਵਿੱਚ ਮਾਰ ਦੇਣਾ ਪਾਪ ਹੈ ?   ਹਾਂ/ਨਹੀਂ
ਜੇਕਰ ਹਾਂ ਤਾਂ ਕੀ ਤੁਸੀ ਫਿਰ ਵੀ ਅਜਿਹਾ ਕਰੋਗੇ ?

```
[handwritten Punjabi response]
```

38.) ਕੀ ਗਰਭਪਾਤ ਕਰਵਾਉਣ ਉਪਰੰਤ ਤੁਹਾਡੀ ਸਿਹਤ ਤੇ ਕੋਈ ਬੁਰਾ ਅਸਰ ਪਿਆ ਹੈ?   ਹਾਂ/ਨਹੀਂ
ਜੇਕਰ ਹਾਂ ਜਾਂ ਤਾਂ ਕੀ ਤਕਲੀਫ ਹੋਈ ?

```
[handwritten Punjabi response]
```

39.) (i) ਜੇਕਰ ਤੁਹਾਡਾ ਪਰਿਵਾਰ ਲੜਕੇ ਲੜਕੀਆਂ ਪੱਖੋ ਤੁਹਾਡੀ ਇੱਛਾ ਅਨੁਸਾਰ ਹੈ ਤਾਂ ਅਜੋਹੇ ਹਾਲਤਾਂ ਵਿਚ ਜੇਕਰ ਤੁਸੀ ਫਿਰ ਗਰਭ ਧਾਰਨ ਕਰਦੇ ਹੋ ਤਾਂ ਕੀ ਤੁਸੀ ਬਿਨਾ ਅਲਟਰਾ ਸਾਊਂਡ ਕਰਵਾਏ ਬੱਚੇ ਨੂੰ ਜਨਮ ਦੇਵੋਗੇ ?   ਹਾਂ/ਨਹੀਂ ✓

(ii) ਜੇਕਰ ਅਲਟਰਾਸਾਊਂਡ ਕਰਵਾਣ ਤੇ ਤੁਹਾਨੂੰ ਪਤਾ ਲਗ ਜਾਏ ਕਿ ਪੇਟ ਵਿਚ ਬੱਚਾ ਲੜਕਾ ਹੈ ਜਾਂ ਲੜਕੀ ਹੈ ਤਾਂ ਤੁਸੀ ਸਫਾਈ ਕਰਵਾਉਗੇ ?
 ਜੇਕਰ ਲੜਕਾ ਹੈ ਤਾਂ   ਹਾਂ/ਨਹੀਂ
 ਜੇਕਰ ਲੜਕੀ ਹੈ ਤਾਂ   ਹਾਂ/ਨਹੀਂ

40.) ਜੇ ਕਰ ਤੁਹਾਡੇ ਲੜਕਾ ਨਹੀਂ ਹੁੰਦਾ ਤਾਂ ਤੁਸੀ :
 ਕਿੰਨੀ ਵਾਰੀ ਕੋਸ਼ਿਸ਼ ਕਰੋਗੇ   1/2/3/4/5 ✓ ਜਾਂ ਜਿਆਦਾ

Annexure - II

Questionnaire

1.) District :
2.) Age of woman :
3.) Married since _____ years
4.) Education :
   a) Illiterate
   b) Primary
   c) Matric
   d) Graduate and Above
5.) Occupation : Housewife / Employed
        If employed then income
6.) Husband's education :
   a) Illiterate
   b) Primary
   c) Matric
   d) Graduate and Above
7.) Financial Status of the family :
    Agriculture Land : 2/5/10/15 acre or above
    Own House   : Kucha/Pucca
    Rooms   : 1-2-3 or more
    Electricity   : Yes / No
    Gas   : Yes / No
    Television   : Yes / No
    Conveyance   : None/Cycle/Scooter/Car/Tractor
    Radio   : Yes / No
    Joint Family   : Yes/ No

Annexure-II

8.) Caste :

9.) Religion :

10.) Do you visit Gurdwara / Temple ?
    Daily / After 1 week / After 1 month / Don't go

11.) No. of living children and age :

Sons

	Age
One	1
Two	2
Three	3

Daughters

One	1
Two	2
Three	3

12.) How many times you have been pregnant _____

13.) Has any child died : Yes/ No

14.) If yes, then :
    Age of child at the time of death _____
    Child was male or female _____
    Reason of death _____

15.) (a) In your view, ideally how many children should be there :
        1/2/3/4 or more
    (b) Amongst those how many should be boys and girls ?
        Boys _____
        Girls _____

16.) Who you think is responsible for the sex of the child.
- God
- Husband
- Wife

17.) Do you know that the sex of a child can be known before birth? Yes / No.
If yes then how ?

_____
_____
_____

18.) From where did you get this information :
- Health Worker
- Husband
- Relative
- Neighbour
- Newspapers/ Advertisements
- Sign Boards

19.) Do you think that one should get to know the sex of the unborn child? Yes/No
State reasons.

_____
_____
_____

20.) Do you think boys are preferred in our society ? Yes / No
If yes, then do you think this discrimination is right? Yes / No
State reasons.

_____
_____
_____
_____

Annexure-II

21.) In your view does the status of a woman increase in the family by having a son ? Yes / No
If yes, then how ?
_____
_____
_____

22.) Is postnatal care better if child is male? Yes / No
If yes, then how ?
_____
_____
_____

23.) What family decisions can you take yourself ?
- What to cook today
- If you fall sick when and from where to get treatment
- When to conceive
- Buying any jewellery / major household items
- For going to your parents' place

24.) In your view what should be the sex of first child : Boy / Girl / Any
State reasons.
_____
_____
_____

25.) Did you get Ultrasound done at the time of first pregnancy to know the sex of your child ? Yes / No

26.) Have you been ill-treated for not giving birth to a male child? Yes / No
If yes, then how ?

_____
_____
_____
_____

27.) To fulfill your desire to have a son, did you go to any saint or adopt any superstitious method ? Yes / No.
If yes, then what did you do ?

_____
_____
_____
_____

28.) Have you undergone any abortion ? Yes/ No
If yes, then
- No. of spontaneous abortions _____
- No. of induced abortions _____
- If induced abortion then state reason :
    - Medical reason
    - Child was female
- Duration of pregnancy at the time of abortion_____
- No. of living sons and daughters at the time of abortion
    - Sons _____
    - Daughters_____

29.) Whether Ultrasound was done before abortion to know the sex of the child.
If yes, who asked you to get it done
- Your own decision
- Husband
- Father-in-law or Mother-in-law
- Parents

Annexure-II

- Friends
- Health Worker
- Any other
  If it was your own decision then state reasons :

  _____
  _____
  _____

30.) How did you feel before getting Ultrasound done for sex determination ?
     Normal / Anxious / Apprehensive

31.) What were your feelings when you came to know that foetus is female ?
     Normal / Sad / Threatened

32.) Did you get abortion done on knowing that the foetus is female ?
     Yes / No
     If yes, then why ?

     _____
     _____
     _____

33.) Who influenced you to get the foetus aborted after knowing the sex ?
   - Your own decision
   - Husband
   - Father-in-law or Mother-in-law
   - Parents
   - Relatives
   - Any other

34.) Were you willing to undergo abortion? Yes / No
If yes, then why?

35.) Any relative in the family who has gone in for female foeticide. Yes / No

36.) Do you regret after foeticide? Yes / No
37.) In your view is it a sin to kill the female foetus. Yes / No
If yes, would you do it again?

38.) Did you undergo any health problems after undergoing abortions? Yes / No
If yes, then what?

39.)(i) If you complete your family i.e. have desired number of children sex-wise and if you conceive would you continue with it as such or go for USG to know the sex of the child. Yes / No
  (ii) If you go for ultra sonography, would you go in for abortion, if you come to know the sex of the unborn child is
    • Male : Yes / No
    • Female : Yes / No
40.) If you don't get a male child, how many times you would try: 1/2/3/4/5 or more

Annexure - III

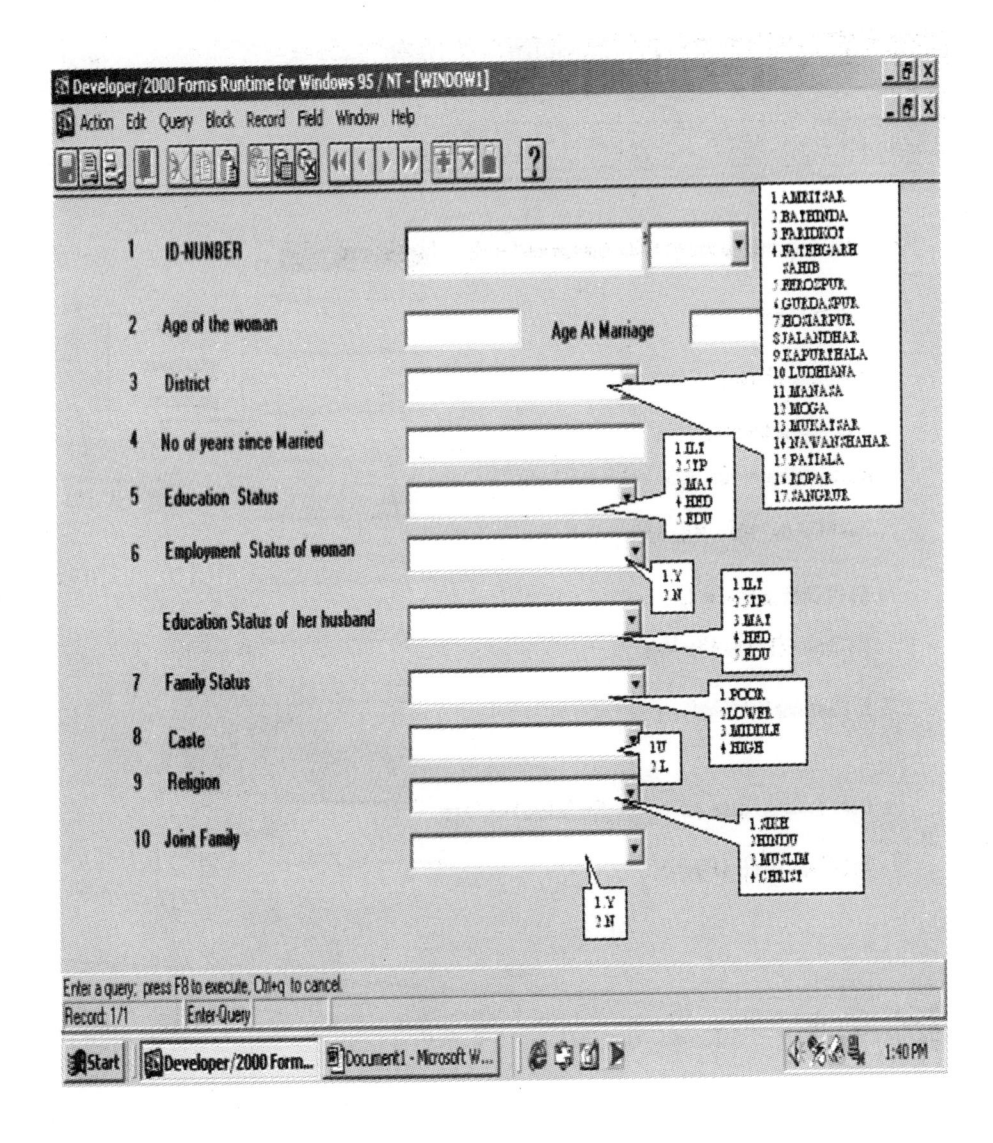

Developer/2000 Forms Runtime for Windows 95 / NT - [WINDOW1]

Action Edit Query Block Record Field Window Help

1	ID-NUMBER		
2	Age of the woman		Age At Marriage
3	District		
4	No of years since Married		
5	Education Status		
6	Employment Status of woman		
	Education Status of her husband		
7	Family Status		
8	Caste		
9	Religion		
10	Joint Family		

District list:
1 AMRITSAR
2 BATHINDA
3 FARIDKOT
4 FATEHGARH SAHIB
5 FEROZPUR
6 GURDASPUR
7 HOSHIARPUR
8 JALANDHAR
9 KAPURTHALA
10 LUDHIANA
11 MANASA
12 MOGA
13 MUKATSAR
14 NAWANSHAHAR
15 PATIALA
16 ROPAR
17 SANGRUR

Education:
1 ILI
2 SIP
3 MAT
4 HED
5 EDU

Employment: 1 Y 2 N

Husband Education:
1 ILI
2 SIP
3 MAT
4 HED
5 EDU

Family Status:
1 POOR
2 LOWER
3 MIDDLE
4 HIGH

Caste: 1 U 2 L

Religion:
1 SIKH
2 HINDU
3 MUSLIM
4 CHRI

Joint Family: 1 Y 2 N

Enter a query; press F8 to execute, Ctrl+q to cancel.
Record: 1/1   Enter-Query

Start | Developer/2000 Form... | Document1 - Microsoft W...   1:40 PM

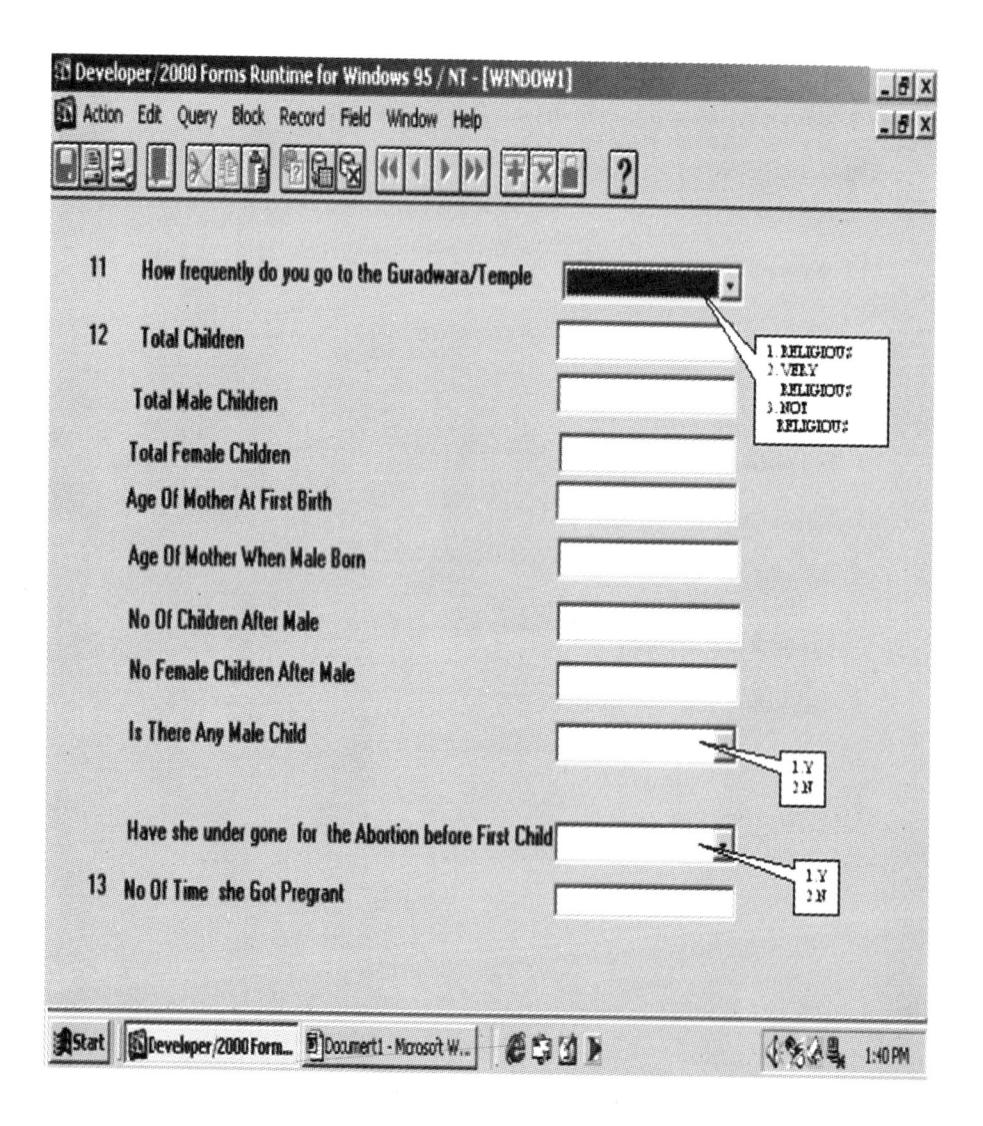

Developer/2000 Forms Runtime for Windows 95 / NT - [WINDOW1]

Action Edit Query Block Record Field Window Help

11	How frequently do you go to the Guradwara/Temple	[▼]	1. RELIGIOUS
			2. VERY RELIGIOUS
12	Total Children		3. NOT RELIGIOUS
	Total Male Children		
	Total Female Children		
	Age Of Mother At First Birth		
	Age Of Mother When Male Born		
	No Of Children After Male		
	No Female Children After Male		
	Is There Any Male Child		1 Y 2 N
	Have she under gone for the Abortion before First Child		1 Y 2 N
13	No Of Time she Got Pregnant		

Annexure-III

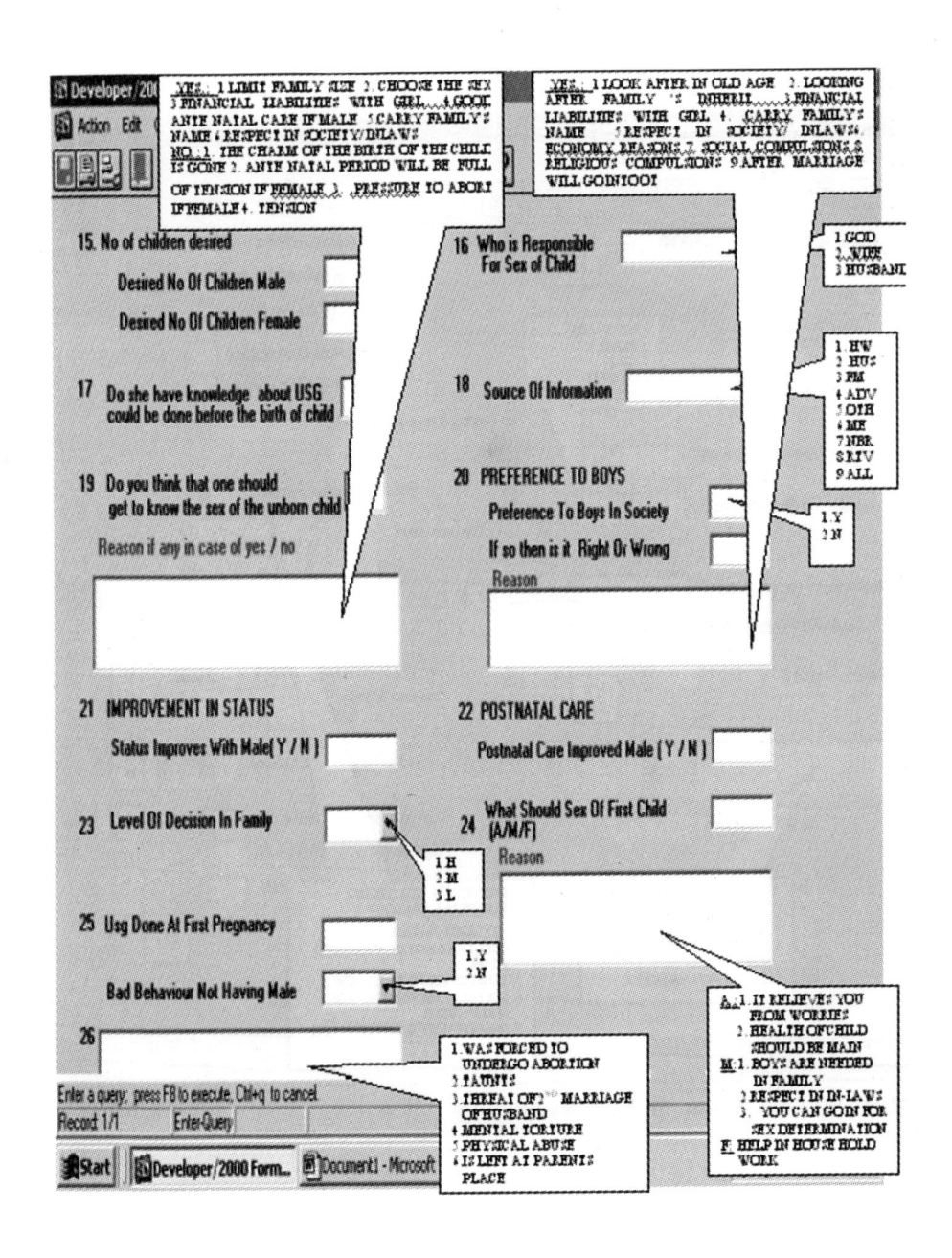

YES: 1 LIMIT FAMILY SIZE 2. CHOOSE THE SEX 3 FINANCIAL LIABILITIES WITH GIRL 4. GOOD ANTE NATAL CARE IF MALE 5 CARRY FAMILY'S NAME 6 RESPECT IN SOCIETY/INLAWS
NO: 1. THE CHARM OF THE BIRTH OF THE CHILD IS GONE 2. ANTE NATAL PERIOD WILL BE FULL OF TENSION IF FEMALE 3. PRESSURE TO ABORT IF FEMALE 4. TENSION

YES: 1 LOOK AFTER IN OLD AGE 2. LOOKING AFTER FAMILY 3. INHERIT FINANCIAL LIABILITIES WITH GIRL 4. CARRY FAMILY'S NAME 5 RESPECT IN SOCIETY INLAWS. ECONOMY REASONS 7. SOCIAL COMPULSIONS 8 RELIGIOUS COMPULSIONS 9 AFTER MARRIAGE WILL GO INTO OT

15. No of children desired
  Desired No Of Children Male
  Desired No Of Children Female

16 Who is Responsible For Sex of Child
  1 GOD
  2 WIFE
  3 HUSBAND

17 Do she have knowledge about USG could be done before the birth of child

18 Source Of Information
  1. HW
  2. HUS
  3. FM
  4. ADV
  5. OTH
  6. ME
  7. NBR
  8. RTV
  9. ALL

19 Do you think that one should get to know the sex of the unborn child
  Reason if any in case of yes / no

20 PREFERENCE TO BOYS
  Preference To Boys In Society
  If so then is it Right Or Wrong
  Reason
  1.Y
  2.N

21 IMPROVEMENT IN STATUS
  Status Improves With Male (Y / N)

22 POSTNATAL CARE
  Postnatal Care Improved Male (Y / N)

23 Level Of Decision In Family
  1 H
  2 M
  3 L

24 What Should Sex Of First Child (A/M/F)
  Reason

25 Usg Done At First Pregnancy
  Bad Behaviour Not Having Male
  1.Y
  2.N

26
  1. WAS FORCED TO UNDERGO ABORTION
  2. TAUNTS
  3. THREAT OF 2ND MARRIAGE OF HUSBAND
  4. MENTAL TORTURE
  5. PHYSICAL ABUSE
  6. IS LEFT AT PARENTS PLACE

  A. 1. IT RELIEVES YOU FROM WORRIES
  2. HEALTH OF CHILD SHOULD BE MAIN
  M: 1. BOYS ARE NEEDED IN FAMILY
  2 RESPECT IN IN-LAWS
  3. YOU CAN GO IN FOR SEX DETERMINATION
  F. HELP IN HOUSE HOLD WORK